small
food

small food

MURDOCH
B O O K S

Contents

Nibbles

Vegetable chips

500 g orange sweet potato
500 g beetroot
500 g parsnip
oil, for deep-frying

Preheat the oven to moderate 180°C (350°F/Gas 4).

Run a vegetable peeler along the length of the sweet potato and beetroot to make thin ribbons. Cut the parsnip into thin slices.

Fill a deep, heavy-based saucepan one-third full of oil and heat to 190°C (375°F), or until a cube of bread dropped into the oil browns in 10 seconds. Cook the vegetables in batches for about 30 seconds, or until golden and crisp, turning with tongs, if necessary. Drain on crumpled paper towels and season with salt. Keep warm on a baking tray in the oven and cook the remaining chips.

Makes a large bowl

Chorizo and tomato salsa

2 tablespoons olive oil
250 g chorizo sausage, finely
  chopped
4 cloves garlic, finely chopped
4 small celery sticks, finely chopped
2 bay leaves
1 red onion, finely chopped
2 teaspoons sweet paprika
6 ripe tomatoes, peeled, seeded,
  chopped
2 tablespoons tomato paste (purée)
2 x 130 g cans corn kernels, drained
1 cup (50 g) fresh coriander leaves,
  roughly chopped
1 tablespoon sugar

Heat the oil in a large frying pan.
Add the sausage, garlic, celery,
bay leaves, onion and paprika.
Cook, stirring, over medium heat
for 10 minutes.

Add the tomato, tomato paste and
corn and cook over high heat for
5 minutes, or until the tomato is
pulpy and the mixture is thick.

Remove the pan from the heat, stir
through the coriander and sugar and
season. Serve hot.

Makes 3 cups

Olive tapenade

400 g Kalamata olives, pitted
2 cloves garlic, crushed
2 anchovy fillets in oil, drained
2 tablespoons capers in brine, rinsed,
    squeezed dry
2 teaspoons chopped fresh thyme
2 teaspoons Dijon mustard
1 tablespoon lemon juice
1/4 cup (60 ml) olive oil
1 tablespoon brandy, optional

Place the Kalamata olives, crushed garlic, anchovies, capers, chopped thyme, Dijon mustard, lemon juice, olive oil and brandy in a food processor and process until smooth. Season to taste with salt and freshly ground black pepper. Spoon into a clean, warm jar, cover with a layer of olive oil, seal and refrigerate for up to 1 week. Serve on bruschetta or with a meze plate.

Makes 1 1/2 cups

Note: When refrigerated, the olive oil may solidify, making it an opaque white colour. This is a property of olive oil and will not affect the flavour of the dish. Simply bring the dish to room temperature before serving and the olive oil with return to a liquid state.

Hint: To make sure your storage jar is very clean, preheat the oven to very slow 120°C (250°F/Gas 1/2). Wash the jar and lid thoroughly in hot soapy water (or preferably in a dishwasher) and rinse well with hot water. Put the jar on a baking tray and place in the oven for 20 minutes, or until fully dry and you are ready to use it. Do not dry the jar or lid with a tea towel.

Crispy Asian noodle pancakes

150 g dried rice vermicelli noodles
¼ cup (15 g) chopped fresh coriander
3 spring onions, finely sliced
1 small red chilli, finely chopped
1 stalk lemon grass, white part only,
  finely chopped
1 clove garlic, crushed
oil, for shallow-frying

Place the noodles in a bowl and cover with boiling water. Stand for 5 minutes, or until soft. Rinse under cold water, drain and dry with paper towels.

Place the noodles in a bowl with the coriander, spring onion, chilli, lemon grass and garlic. Season to taste with salt and mix.

Heat the oil in a heavy-based pan and shallow-fry 2 tablespoons of the mixture in hot oil. Flatten with a spatula while cooking and fry until crisp and golden on both sides. Drain the pancakes on paper towels and sprinkle with salt.

Makes about 25

Warm crab and lemon dip

80 g butter
2 cloves garlic, crushed
3 French shallots, thinly sliced
1 teaspoon mustard powder
$\frac{1}{2}$ teaspoon cayenne pepper
$\frac{1}{2}$ cup (125 ml) cream
150 g cream cheese
$\frac{1}{2}$ cup (60 g) grated Cheddar
350 g can crab meat, drained
2 tablespoons lemon juice
2 teaspoons Worcestershire sauce
3 teaspoons chopped fresh tarragon
$\frac{1}{2}$ cup (40 g) fresh breadcrumbs
1 tablespoon chopped fresh parsley

Preheat the oven to warm 170°C (325°F/Gas 3).

Melt half the butter in a saucepan, then cook the garlic and shallots for 2–3 minutes, or until just softened. Add the mustard powder, cayenne pepper and cream. Bring to a simmer and slowly whisk in the cream cheese, a little at a time. When the cream cheese is completely incorporated, whisk in the Cheddar and allow to cook, stirring constantly, over very low heat for 1–2 minutes, or until smooth. Remove from the heat and add the crab meat, lemon juice, Worcestershire sauce and 2 teaspoons of the tarragon. Season to taste with salt and freshly cracked black pepper. Mix, then transfer to a small baking dish.

Melt the remaining butter in a small saucepan, add the breadcrumbs, chopped parsley and remaining tarragon and stir until just combined. Sprinkle over the crab mixture and bake for 15 minutes, or until golden. Serve warm.

Makes 2$\frac{1}{2}$ cups

Parmesan wafers

1¼ cups (125 g) good-quality grated
  Parmesan
1 tablespoon plain flour
2 tablespoons fresh thyme

Preheat the oven to hot 220°C
(425°F/Gas 7). Line two baking trays
with baking paper and, using a 7 cm
cutter as a guide, draw circles on the
paper. Turn the paper upside down
on the trays.

Toss the cheese and flour together
in a bowl, then sprinkle 2 teaspoons
of the mixture over 3–4 circles on the
paper, spreading the mixture to the
edge of each round. Scatter a few
thyme leaves over each round.

Bake in batches for about 3 minutes,
or until melted but not firm. Using a
spatula, turn the rounds over and
cook for a minute more, or until they
are firm and light golden. Remove
each round from the tray and drape
over a rolling pin or bottle until cool.
Repeat with the rest of the
ingredients.

Makes 30

Spinach pâté

400 g English spinach
30 g butter
1/2 teaspoon ground coriander
pinch cayenne pepper
2 spring onions, roughly chopped
1 clove garlic
1/3 cup (50 g) blanched almonds
2 teaspoons white wine vinegar
1/2 cup (125 g) sour cream

Remove the stems from the spinach. Wash the leaves and place wet in a pan. Cover and cook for 2 minutes, or until wilted, then drain, reserving 1/4 cup (60 ml) of the cooking liquid. Cool the spinach then squeeze dry.

Melt the butter in a small pan. Add the coriander, cayenne pepper, spring onion, garlic and almonds, and cook until the onion is tender. Cool.

Place in a food processor and process until finely chopped. Add the spinach and process, gradually adding the reserved cooking liquid and vinegar.

Stir in the sour cream and season well with salt and pepper.

Makes 1 1/2 cups

Seasoned popcorn

¼ cup (60 ml) oil
²/₃ cup (150 g) popping corn
40 g butter
²/₃ cup (125 g) finely chopped
  Kalamata olives
1 bird's eye chilli, finely chopped
1 clove garlic, crushed
1 tablespoon chopped fresh parsley
1 tablespoon chopped fresh oregano
1 teaspoon grated lemon zest

Heat the oil in a large saucepan, add the popping corn and cover. Cook over medium heat, shaking occasionally, until the popping stops. Transfer to a large bowl and discard any unpopped corn.

Melt the butter in a large frying pan and add the remaining ingredients. Mix, then toss through the popcorn. Serve warm.

Makes a large bowl

Greek-style feta and yoghurt dip

250 g mild feta cheese
250 g ricotta cheese
2 tablespoons olive oil
3 cloves garlic, crushed
1 tablespoon lemon juice
1/4 teaspoon cayenne pepper
3/4 cup (185 g) Greek-style yoghurt
1/3 cup (20 g) chopped fresh mint
1 teaspoon chopped fresh oregano
1/4 cup (30 g) pitted black olives, diced
1 small tomato, finely diced
1–2 teaspoons lemon zest, thinly
   sliced

Purée the feta, ricotta, oil, garlic,
lemon juice, cayenne pepper and half
the yoghurt in a blender or food
processor until smooth. Stir in the
remaining yoghurt, mint and oregano.

Transfer the dip to a serving bowl
and top with the olives, tomato and
lemon zest.

Makes 4 cups

Cheese sticks

1¼ cups (155 g) plain flour
100 g unsalted butter, chilled and
  chopped
¾ cup (100 g) grated Gruyère
1 tablespoon finely chopped fresh
  oregano
1 egg yolk
1 tablespoon sea salt flakes

Line two baking trays with baking paper. Put the flour and butter in a food processor and process in short bursts until the mixture resembles fine breadcrumbs. Add the Gruyère and oregano and process for 10 seconds, or until just combined. Add the egg yolk and about 1 tablespoon water, and process until the dough just comes together.

Turn the dough out onto a lightly floured surface and gather into a ball. Form 2 teaspoons of dough into a ball, then roll out into a stick about 12 cm (5 inches) long and place on the baking trays. Repeat with the remaining dough, then cover with plastic wrap and refrigerate for 15–20 minutes. Preheat the oven to moderately hot 200°C (400°F/Gas 6).

Lightly brush the sticks with water and sprinkle with the sea salt flakes. Bake for 10 minutes, or until golden. Cool on a wire rack and serve with dips or as part of an antipasto platter.

Makes 30

Storage: Cheese sticks will keep for up to 1 week in an airtight container.

Spicy poppadoms

3 green cardamom seeds
1½ tablespoons coriander seeds
1 tablespoon cumin seeds
2 cloves
1 teaspoon black peppercorns
1 bay leaf, crushed
1 teaspoon ground mace
¼ teaspoon ground cinnamon
pinch of ground chilli
oil, for deep-frying
24 large poppadoms, broken into
  quarters

Toast the cardamom, coriander and cumin seeds, cloves, peppercorns and bay leaf in a dry frying pan over low heat for 2–3 minutes, or until richly fragrant. Cool for 5 minutes, then grind to a fine powder. Stir in the mace, cinnamon and chilli.

Fill a wide, large saucepan one-third full with oil and heat to 180°C (350°F), or until a cube of bread dropped into the oil browns in 15 seconds. Deep-fry the pieces of poppadom, a few at a time, until crisp and golden. Drain on crumpled paper towels and sprinkle with the spice mix while still hot.

Makes a large bowl

Corn salsa with cumin

3 corn cobs
2 tablespoons olive oil
2 teaspoons ground cumin
2 jalapeño chillies, stems and seeds
  removed, diced
1/4 cup (40 g) semi-dried tomatoes,
  diced
2 tablespoons lime juice
1/4 cup (7 g) fresh coriander leaves,
  finely chopped
3 spring onions, finely chopped

Preheat the oven to moderately hot 200°C (400°F/Gas 6). Cut the kernels from the corn with a sharp knife — you will need 2 cups (400 g).

Combine the corn with the oil, cumin, chilli and 1/4 cup (60 ml) water, and place in a baking dish. Cook in the oven for 30 minutes, or until the corn begins to brown slightly.

Combine the corn with the tomato, lime juice, coriander and spring onion. Season.

Makes 1 1/2 cups

Two-seed crackers

2 cups (250 g) plain flour
1 teaspoon baking powder
2 tablespoons poppy seeds
2 tablespoons sesame seeds
60 g butter, chilled and chopped
1/2 cup (125 ml) iced water

Preheat the oven to moderate 180°C (350°F/Gas 4). Line two baking trays with baking paper, or brush lightly with oil. Sift the flour, baking powder and 1/2 teaspoon salt into a bowl. Add the seeds and season with pepper. Stir to combine. Rub the butter into the flour with your fingertips until the mixture resembles fine breadcrumbs.

Make a well in the centre and add almost all the water. Mix together with a flat-bladed knife using a cutting action, adding the remaining water if necessary, until the mixture comes together in soft beads.

Gather the dough into a rough ball. Handle the dough gently, and do not knead it. Divide the dough into two portions. Place one portion between two sheets of baking paper and roll to a thickness of 2 mm. Cover the other portion with plastic wrap until needed.

Using a 6 cm round cutter, cut rounds from the dough. Prick all over with a fork and transfer to the baking trays. Repeat with the remaining dough. Pile any dough trimmings together (do not knead) and gently re-roll. Cut out more rounds. Bake for 20–25 minutes, or until lightly golden. Transfer to a wire rack to cool. Store in an airtight container for up to 5 days.

Makes 30

White bean dip

2 x 400 g cans lima or cannellini
   beans, drained and rinsed
½ cup (125 ml) olive oil
⅓ cup (80 ml) lemon juice
3 cloves garlic, finely chopped
1 tablespoon finely chopped fresh
   rosemary

Place the beans in a food processor
with the oil, lemon juice, garlic and
rosemary and 1 teaspoon salt.
Process until smooth, then season
with cracked black pepper.

Makes 3 cups

Note: This dip improves with age, so
you can make it up to 2 days ahead
of time.

Tortilla shards

2 tablespoons sweet paprika
1/4 teaspoon cayenne pepper
oil, for deep-frying
8 large flour tortillas, cut into long
   triangles

Combine the paprika and cayenne pepper in a small bowl.

Fill a deep heavy-based saucepan one-third full of oil and heat to 180°C (350°F), or until a cube of bread dropped into the oil browns in 15 seconds. Drop the tortilla shards in the oil in batches and deep-fry until crisp. Drain on crumpled paper towels and sprinkle lightly with the paprika mix while still hot.

Serves 8–10

Basil and cheese grissini

7 g sachet dry yeast
1 teaspoon sugar
4 cups (500 g) plain flour
1/4 cup (60 ml) olive oil
1/4 cup (15 g) chopped fresh basil
1/2 cup (50 g) finely grated Parmesan
2 teaspoons sea salt flakes

Combine the yeast, sugar and
1 1/4 cups (315 ml) warm water in a
bowl and leave in a warm place for
5–10 minutes, or until foamy. Sift the
flour and 1 teaspoon salt into a bowl.
Stir the yeast and oil into the flour to
form a dough, adding a little more
water if necessary.

Gently gather the dough into a ball
and turn out onto a lightly floured
surface. Knead for 10 minutes, or
until soft and elastic. Add the basil
and Parmesan, and knead for
1–2 minutes to incorporate evenly.

Place the dough in a lightly oiled bowl
and cover with plastic wrap. Leave
in a warm place for 1 hour, or until
doubled in volume. Preheat the oven
to very hot 230°C (450°F/Gas 8) and
lightly grease two large baking trays.

Punch down the dough and knead
for 1 minute. Divide into 24 portions,
and roll each portion into a 30 cm
long stick. Place on the trays and
brush with water. Sprinkle with the
salt flakes. Bake for 15 minutes, or
until crisp and golden.

Makes 24

Curried nuts

500 g mixed nuts (almonds, brazil
nuts, pecans, macadamias, cashew
nuts)
1 egg white
2 tablespoons curry powder
1 teaspoon ground cumin

Preheat the oven to slow 150°C
(300°F/Gas 2). Spread the nuts in
a single layer on a baking tray and
roast for 10 minutes.

Whisk the egg white until frothy, then
add the nuts, curry powder, cumin
and 1 teaspoon salt. Toss together
and return to the oven for a further
10–15 minutes, then allow to cool.

Makes 4 1/2 cups

Aïoli with crudités

Aïoli
4 garlic cloves, crushed
2 egg yolks
1¼ cups (315 ml) light olive or
  vegetable oil
1 tablespoon lemon juice
pinch of ground white pepper

12 asparagus spears, trimmed
12 radishes, trimmed
½ telegraph cucumber, seeded,
  halved lengthways and cut into
  batons
1 head of witlof (chicory), leaves
  separated

For the aïoli, place the garlic, egg yolks and a pinch of salt in a food processor and process for 10 seconds. With the motor running, add the oil in a thin, slow stream. The mixture will start to thicken. When this happens you can add the oil a little faster. Process until all the oil is incorporated and the mixture is thick and creamy. Stir in the lemon juice and white pepper.

Bring a saucepan of water to the boil, add the asparagus and cook for 1 minute. Remove and plunge into a bowl of iced water.

Arrange the asparagus, radish, cucumber and witlof decoratively on a platter and place the aïoli in a bowl on the platter. The aïoli can also be used as a sandwich spread or as a sauce for chicken or fish.

Serves 4

Note: It is important that all the ingredients are at room temperature when making this recipe. Should the aïoli start to curdle, beat in 1–2 teaspoons boiling water. If this fails, put another egg yolk in a clean bowl and very slowly whisk the curdled mixture into it, one drop at a time, then continue as above.

Mixed Asian crisps

oil, for deep-frying
16 cassava crackers, broken into
small pieces (see Note)
16 round won ton wrappers
16 small uncooked plain prawn
crackers
1 sheet toasted nori, shredded

Fill a deep heavy-based saucepan or deep-fryer one-third full of oil and heat to 180°C (350°F), or until a cube of bread dropped into the oil browns in 15 seconds.

Deep-fry the cassava pieces until crisp. Remove with a slotted spoon and drain on crumpled paper towels. Repeat with the won ton wrappers and prawn chips.

When they are all cool, combine and toss with the nori.

Makes a large bowl

Note: Cassava crackers are made from the flour of the dried cassava root. Available from Asian food stores.

Guacamole

2 large ripe avocados
2 tablespoons lime juice
1 tomato, seeded and finely diced
1 red chilli, finely chopped
2 tablespoons finely diced red onion
1 1/2 tablespoons chopped fresh
  coriander leaves
1 1/2 tablespoons sour cream
1 tablespoon olive oil
1/2 teaspoon ground cumin
pinch of cayenne pepper

Put the avocado and lime juice in
a large bowl, then mash. Stir in the
diced tomato, chilli, onion, coriander,
sour cream, olive oil and cumin.
Season with cayenne pepper and
some salt and pepper.

Spoon into a serving bowl and
sprinkle with cayenne pepper.

Makes 2 cups

Pizza wheels

½ small red capsicum (peppers),
  finely chopped
¼ cup (15 g) chopped fresh parsley
2 tablespoons chopped fresh oregano
100 g finely chopped ham or salami
½ cup (60 g) grated Cheddar
¼ cup (60 g) tomato paste (purée)
2 sheets ready-rolled puff pastry,
  thawed

Preheat the oven to moderately hot 200°C (400°F/Gas 6).

Combine the capsicum, parsley, oregano, ham and cheese in a bowl.

Spread the tomato paste onto each sheet of pastry, leaving a 2 cm border along one side, and sprinkle the capsicum mixture over the top. Roll up the pastry to enclose the filling, leaving the plain edge until last. Brush the edge lightly with water and fold over to seal.

Cut each roll into 1 cm rounds and place onto greased oven trays. Bake for 20 minutes, or until golden.

Makes 48

Hummus

1 cup (220 g) dried chickpeas
2 tablespoons tahini
4 cloves garlic, crushed
2 teaspoons ground cumin
1/3 cup (80 ml) lemon juice
3 tablespoons olive oil
large pinch cayenne pepper
extra lemon juice, optional
extra olive oil, to garnish
paprika, to garnish
chopped fresh parsley, to garnish

Soak the chickpeas in 1 litre water overnight. Drain and place in a large saucepan with 2 litres fresh water (enough to cover the chickpeas by 5 cm). Bring to the boil, then reduce the heat and simmer for 1 hour 15 minutes, or until the chickpeas are very tender. Skim any scum from the surface. Drain well, reserve the cooking liquid and leave until cool enough to handle. Pick over for any loose skins and discard.

Process the chickpeas, tahini, garlic, cumin, lemon juice, olive oil, cayenne pepper and 1 1/2 teaspoons salt in a food processor until thick and smooth. With the motor still running, gradually add enough reserved cooking liquid (about 3/4 cup/185 ml) to form a smooth creamy purée. Season with salt or extra lemon juice.

Spread onto a flat bowl or plate, drizzle with oil, sprinkle with paprika and scatter the parsley over the top. Serve with pitta bread or pide.

Makes 3 cups

Cheese, olive and sun-dried tomato toasts

2 cups (250 g) self-raising flour
1 cup (125 g) grated Cheddar
1/4 cup (25 g) freshly grated Parmesan
1/3 cup (50 g) pine nuts
1 cup (250 ml) milk
1 egg, lightly beaten
30 g butter, melted
1/2 cup (60 g) pitted black olives,
  chopped
1/4 cup (40 g) sun-dried tomatoes,
  finely chopped
1/3 cup (40 g) grated Cheddar, extra

Preheat the oven to moderately hot 200°C (400°F/Gas 6). Lightly grease two 8 x 26 cm bar tins and cover the bases with non-stick baking paper. Combine the flour, cheeses and pine nuts in a bowl. Make a well in the centre of the mixture.

Pour in the combined milk, egg, butter, olives and sun-dried tomato, and stir to form a slightly sticky dough.

Divide the mixture between the tins. Smooth the surface and sprinkle with the extra cheese. Bake for 45 minutes, or until cooked through when tested with a skewer. Leave in the tins for 5 minutes, then turn onto wire racks to cool.

Cut into 5 mm slices and place on baking trays lined with baking paper. Bake for 15–20 minutes, or until the toasts are golden and crisp.

Makes about 50

Broad bean dip

1 cup (200 g) dried broad beans
(fava or ful nabed — see Note)
2 cloves garlic, crushed
¼ teaspoon ground cumin
1½ tablespoons lemon juice
up to 75 ml olive oil
2 tablespoons chopped fresh
flat-leaf parsley
flatbread, for serving

Rinse the beans well, then place in a bowl and cover with 2 cups (500 ml) of water and leave to soak overnight.

If using peeled beans (see Note), transfer them and their soaking water to a large heavy-based saucepan. If using unpeeled beans, drain, then add to the pan with 2 cups (500 ml) fresh water. Bring to the boil, cover, and simmer for 5–6 hours. Check the water level from time to time and add a little boiling water, as necessary, to keep the beans moist. Do not stir, but shake the pan occasionally to prevent sticking. Set aside to cool slightly.

Purée the contents of the pan in a food processor, then transfer to a bowl and stir in the garlic, cumin and lemon juice. Gradually stir in enough olive oil to give a dipping consistency. As the mixture cools it may become thick, in which case you can stir in a little warm water to return the mixture to dipping consistency.

Spread over a large dish and sprinkle with the parsley. Serve with the flatbread, cut into triangles.

Serves 6

Note: The fava beans can be the ready-peeled white ones or the small, brown ones.

Potato skins

6 large potatoes, unpeeled
oil, for deep-frying

Preheat the oven to hot 210°C (415°F/Gas 6–7). Prick each potato with a fork and bake for 1 hour, or until the skins are crisp and the flesh is soft. Turn once during cooking.

Leave the potatoes to cool, then halve them and scoop out the flesh, leaving a thin layer of potato in each shell. Cut each half into 3 wedges.

Fill a deep heavy-based pan one-third full of oil and heat to 190°C (375°F). or until a cube of bread browns in 10 seconds. Cook the potato skins in batches for 2–3 minutes, or until crisp. Drain on paper towels. Sprinkle with salt and pepper.

Makes 36

Prawn and green chilli pâté

100 g butter
2 cloves garlic, crushed
1 small green chilli, seeded and
  chopped
750 g raw prawns, peeled and
  deveined
1 teaspoon finely grated lime zest
1 tablespoon lime juice
2 tablespoons whole-egg mayonnaise
2 tablespoons chopped fresh
  coriander
Tabasco sauce, to taste (optional)

Melt the butter in a large frying pan
and add the garlic, chilli and prawns.
Cook over medium heat for
20 minutes, or until tender.

Place the prawn mixture into a food
processor, add the lime zest and juice
and process until roughly chopped.
Stir through the mayonnaise and
coriander and season with Tabasco
sauce, salt and pepper. Spoon into
a serving dish.

Chill for at least 1 hour or until firm.
Allow the pâté to return to room
temperature before serving.

Makes 1$^2/_3$ cups

Spiced soy crackers

1¼ cups (155 g) plain flour
¾ cup (70 g) soy flour
½ teaspoon garam masala
½ teaspoon paprika
2½ tablespoons olive oil
2½ tablespoons lemon juice

Place the flours, garam masala, paprika and ½ teaspoon salt in a food processor. Add the oil, lemon juice and 100 ml water and blend until the mixture comes together in a ball. Cover in plastic wrap and place in the refrigerator for 1 hour.

Preheat the oven to warm 160°C (315°F/Gas 2–3). Line 3 baking trays with baking paper. Cut the dough into 5 or 6 pieces, then roll each piece into rectangles as thinly as possible—about 2 mm thick. Cut each piece into long thin triangles (4 x 10 cm). Place on the prepared trays.

Bake for 20 minutes, or until crisp and lightly coloured. Serve with your favourite dip.

Makes 24

Baba ghannouj
(Turkish eggplant dip)

2 eggplants (aubergine) (1 kg)
3 cloves garlic, crushed
½ teaspoon ground cumin
⅓ cup (80 ml) lemon juice
2 tablespoons tahini
pinch cayenne pepper
1½ tablespoons olive oil
1 tablespoon finely chopped
   fresh flat-leaf parsley
black olives, to garnish

Preheat the oven to moderately hot 200°C (400°F/Gas 6). Pierce the eggplants several times with a fork, then cook over an open flame for about 5 minutes, or until the skin is black and blistering, then place in a roasting tin and bake for 45 minutes, or until the eggplants are very soft and wrinkled. Place in a colander over a bowl to drain off any bitter juices and leave to stand for 30 minutes, or until cool.

Carefully peel the skin from the eggplant, chop the flesh and place in a food processor with the garlic, cumin, lemon, tahini, cayenne and olive oil. Process until smooth and creamy. Alternatively, use a potato masher or fork. Season with salt and stir in the parsley. Spread onto a flat bowl or plate and garnish with the olives. Serve with flatbread or pide.

Makes 1¾ cups

Note: If you prefer, you can roast the eggplant in a moderately hot 200°C (400°F/Gas 6) oven for 1 hour, or until very soft and wrinkled.

Fried chickpeas

1 1/4 cups (275 g) dried chickpeas
oil, for deep-frying
1/2 teaspoon paprika
1/4 teaspoon cayenne pepper

Soak the chickpeas overnight in plenty of cold water. Drain well and pat dry with paper towels.

Fill a deep saucepan one-third full of oil and heat to 180°C (350°F), or until a cube of bread dropped into the hot oil browns in 15 seconds. Deep-fry half the chickpeas for 3 minutes. Remove with a slotted spoon, drain on crumpled paper towels and repeat with the rest of the chickpeas. Partially cover the saucepan as some of the chickpeas may pop. Don't leave the oil unattended.

Deep-fry the chickpeas again in batches for 3 minutes each batch, or until browned. Drain well again on crumpled paper towels. Combine the paprika and cayenne pepper with a little salt and sprinkle the mixture over the hot chickpeas. Allow to cool before serving.

Makes a large bowl

Taramosalata

5 slices white bread, crusts removed
1/3 cup (80 ml) milk
100 g can tarama (mullet roe)
1 egg yolk
1/2 small onion, grated
1 clove garlic, crushed
2 tablespoons lemon juice
1/3 cup (80 ml) olive oil
pinch ground white pepper

Soak the bread in the milk for
10 minutes. Press in a strainer to
extract any excess milk, then place
in a food processor with the tarama,
egg yolk, onion and garlic. Process
for 30 seconds, or until smooth, then
add 1 tablespoon lemon juice.

With the motor running, slowly pour
in the olive oil. The mixture should be
smooth and of a dipping consistency.
Add the remaining lemon juice and
a pinch of white pepper. If the dip
tastes too salty, add another piece
of bread.

Makes 1 1/2 cups

Variation: Try smoked cod's roe
instead of the mullet roe.

Marinated olives

150 g Kalamata olives
150 g good-quality green olives
3/4 cup (185 ml) extra virgin olive oil
2 sprigs fresh rosemary
1/2 tablespoon fresh thyme leaves
2 small red chillies, seeded
several strips lemon peel
2 garlic cloves, bruised
1/2 teaspoon fennel seeds
2 fresh thyme sprigs, extra

Place the olives, oil, rosemary, thyme, chillies, lemon peel, garlic and fennel in a large saucepan and warm over low heat. Transfer to a bowl and marinate overnight at room temperature.

Remove the olives from the oil with a slotted spoon and discard the herbs, reserving the oil. Add the extra thyme to the olives before serving.

Makes 2 cups

Note: Serve the oil with bread.

Hot Italian Bolognaise dip

1 tablespoon olive oil
1 onion, finely choppped
2 cloves garlic, chopped
300 g minced beef
425 g can chopped tomatoes
3 tablespoons tomato paste
1 tablespoon chopped fresh basil
1 tablespoon chopped fresh parsley
sour cream, to serve

Heat the oil in a frying pan, add the onion and garlic and cook, stirring occasionally, over medium heat for 3 minutes, or until the onion is soft. Add the beef and cook, stirring, for 5 minutes, or until browned, pressing with a spoon or the back of a fork to remove any lumps.

Add the tomato, tomato paste and basil. Bring to the boil, then reduce the heat and simmer for 15 minutes. Stir in the parsley and season to taste with salt and pepper.

Serve hot, topped with a generous dollop of sour cream.

Makes 3 cups

Note: This dip can also be served in a cob loaf. Eat straight away so the bread stays crispy.

Pepper and almond bread

2 teaspoons black peppercorns
2 egg whites
1/3 cup (90 g) caster sugar
3/4 cup (90 g) plain flour
1/4 teaspoon ground ginger
1/4 teaspoon ground cinnamon
1 cup (155 g) almonds

Preheat the oven to moderate 180°C (350°F/Gas 4). Grease an 8 x 26 cm bar tin and line the base and sides with baking paper. Lightly crush the peppercorns with the back of a metal spoon or in a mortar and pestle.

Beat the egg whites and sugar with electric beaters for 4 minutes, or until the mixture turns white and thickens. Sift the flour, ginger and cinnamon and fold in with the almonds and crushed peppercorns.

Spread the mixture into the tin. Bake for 35 minutes, or until lightly browned. Cool in the tin for at least 3 hours, before turning out onto a board. (At this stage, you can wrap the bread in foil and slice the next day.) Using a serrated knife, cut the bread into 3 mm slices. Place the slices in a single layer on baking trays. Bake in a slow 150°C (300°F/Gas 2) oven for about 25–35 minutes, or until the slices are dry and crisp. Allow to cool completely before serving.

Makes about 70 pieces

Note: To make traditional almond bread, simply remove the peppercorns.

Herb cheese log

500 g cream cheese, softened
1 tablespoon lemon juice
1 clove garlic, crushed
2 teaspoons chopped fresh thyme
2 teaspoons chopped fresh tarragon
1 tablespoon chopped fresh
 flat-leaf parsley
1 cup (50 g) snipped fresh chives

Put the cream cheese in a large bowl and beat with electric beaters until soft and creamy. Mix in the lemon juice and garlic. In a separate bowl, combine the thyme, tarragon and chopped parsley.

Line a 20 x 30 cm tin with foil. Spread the chives over the base of the tin, then spoon the cream cheese mixture over the chives. Using a palette knife, gently spread the mixture into the tin, pushing it into any gaps. Sprinkle the combined herbs evenly over the top.

Lift the foil from the tin and place on a work surface. Roll the cheese into a log, starting from the longest edge, then cover and place on a baking tray. Refrigerate for at least 3 hours, or preferably overnight.

Makes a 30 cm log

Honey-roasted peanuts

350 g raw shelled peanuts
1/2 cup (175 g) honey
1 1/2 teaspoons Chinese five-spice
   powder

Preheat the oven to slow 150°C
(300°F/Gas 2).

Combine the ingredients in a small
saucepan and warm over low heat.

Spread the nuts onto a large baking
tray lined with baking paper and bake
for 15–20 minutes, or until golden
brown. Cool before serving.

Makes 2 1/2 cups

Storage: You can store the honey-
roasted peanuts in an airtight
container for up to 1 week.

Warm lentil dip

2/3 cup (160 g) red lentils
1 tablespoon olive oil
1 onion, chopped
2 cloves garlic, crushed
2 teaspoons grated fresh ginger
1/2 teaspoon ground turmeric
1 teaspoon ground cumin
400 g can chopped tomatoes
1 tablespoon chopped fresh coriander

Wash the lentils under cold running water and drain well. Heat the oil in a large frying pan. Add the onion, garlic and ginger and cook over medium heat for 3–4 minutes, or until the onion is soft and translucent.

Add the turmeric, cumin and lentils and cook, stirring, for 1 minute, or until fragrant. Add 1 cup (250 ml) water and the undrained tomatoes to the mixture and bring to the boil, then reduce the heat and simmer for about 20 minutes, or until the lentils are soft.

Transfer the mixture to a food processor and process until well combined. Add the coriander, season and process until combined.

Makes 2 cups

Herbed lavash

½ cup (125 ml) olive oil
3 cloves garlic, crushed
6 slices lavash bread
2 teaspoons sea salt flakes
2 teaspoons dried mixed Italian herbs

Preheat the oven to moderate 180°C (350°F/Gas 4).

Heat the oil and garlic in a small saucepan over low heat until the oil is warm and the garlic is fragrant but not browned.

Brush the lavash bread on both sides with the garlic oil. Cut each piece of bread into eight triangular wedges and position side-by-side on baking trays. Sprinkle the upper side with the sea salt and herbs. Bake the lavash for 8–10 minutes, or until crisp.

Makes about 48 pieces

Pork and peanut dip

Paste
2 small dried red chillies
2 teaspoons chopped fresh coriander
   root
3 teaspoons ground white pepper
6 cloves garlic, chopped
4 red Asian shallots, chopped

1 tablespoon peanut oil
300 g pork mince
2 fresh kaffir lime leaves
1 cup (250 ml) coconut cream
1/3 cup (50 g) peanuts, toasted and
   chopped
1 1/2 tablespoons lime juice
3 tablespoons fish sauce
2 tablespoons grated palm sugar
1 tablespoon finely shredded fresh
   Thai basil or coriander leaves
peanut oil, for deep-frying
150 g Cassava crackers

Soak the chillies in boiling water and
for 15 minutes. Remove the seeds
and chop. Blend all of the paste
ingredients in a food processor until
smooth — add water if necessary.

Heat the oil in a saucepan. Add the
paste and cook, stirring frequently,
over medium heat, for 15 minutes,
or until the paste darkens. Add the
mince and stir for 5 minutes, or until
coloured. Gradually add the lime
leaves and coconut cream, scraping
the base of the pan. Cook for
40 minutes, stirring frequently, until
the liquid has almost evaporated.
Add the peanuts, lime juice, fish sauce
and sugar, and cook for 10 minutes,
or until the oil begins to separate.
Remove from the heat, discard the
lime leaves and stir in the basil.

Fill a deep heavy-based saucepan
one-third full of oil and heat to 180°C
(350°F), or until a cube of bread
browns in 15 seconds. Break the
crackers in half. Deep-fry in small
batches until pale, golden and puffed.
Remove immediately and drain. Serve
with the dip.

Serves 6–8

Note: Cassava crackers are available
from Asian food stores.

Dukkah

1/3 cup (50 g) sesame seeds
1 tablespoon coriander seeds
2 teaspoons cumin seeds
1 teaspoon ground cumin
pinch fennel seeds
1/2 teaspoon sea salt
1/2 teaspoon ground black
  peppercorns
1/2 cup (80 g) blanched almonds,
  toasted

Combine the seeds, spices, salt and peppercorns in a pan. Stir over low heat for 5 minutes, or until the seeds are toasted. Cool completely.

Combine the almonds and seed mixture in the bowl of a food processor and process until the mixture resembles a coarse powder.

Serve with Turkish bread and olive oil for dipping.

Makes 3/4 cup

Green Mexican salsa

300 g can tomatillos, drained
  (see Note)
1 small onion, chopped
1 jalapeño chilli, finely chopped
3 cloves garlic, crushed
2 tablespoons chopped fresh
  coriander leaves
1–2 teaspoons lime juice

Place the tomatillos in a food
processor with the onion, chilli, garlic
and 1 tablespoon of the coriander.
Process until smooth, then blend in
the lime juice to taste. Add the rest
of the coriander and process just long
enough to mix it through the dip.

Makes 2 cups

Note: Tomatillos resemble green
tomatoes with a papery husk and are
extensively used in Mexican cooking.

Corn chips

4 corn tortillas
oil, for deep-frying

Cut each tortilla into 8 pieces.

Fill a heavy-based saucepan one-third full of oil and heat to 190°C (375°F) or until a cube of bread dropped into the hot oil browns in 10 seconds. Cook the corn tortillas in batches for 1–2 minutes, or until crisp and golden. Drain on crumpled paper towels. Sprinkle with salt, if desired.

Makes 32

Mini Indian yoghurt bread

1 x 280 g packet Naan bread mix
2 spring onions, finely chopped
1 cup (250 g) plain yoghurt
1 tablespoon nigella seeds (kalonji)

Preheat the oven to moderately hot 190°C (375°F/Gas 5). Empty the bread mix into a bowl and add the chopped spring onion. Follow the manufacturer's instructions to make the dough.

Divide the dough into 4 portions, then each portion into 6. On a lightly floured surface, roll each piece out to a 5 cm round.

Place the rounds on lightly greased oven trays. Top with a teaspoon of yoghurt, spread roughly, then sprinkle with the nigella seeds. Leave for 5 minutes. Bake for 15 minutes, or until golden brown and crisp.

Makes 24

Warm cheese dip

40 g butter
3 spring onions, finely chopped
2 jalapeño chillies, finely chopped
½ teaspoon ground cumin
¾ cup (185 g) sour cream
2 cups (250 g) grated Cheddar
green Tabasco sauce, to drizzle

Melt the butter in a saucepan and add the spring onion, chilli and cumin. Cook without browning over low heat, stirring often, for 6–8 minutes.

Stir in the sour cream and, when it is warm, add the Cheddar. Stir constantly until the cheese melts and the mixture is glossy and smooth. Transfer to a bowl, drizzle with a little Tabasco and serve warm.

Makes 2 cups

Spicy chicken goujons

3 chicken breast fillets
plain flour, for coating
oil, for deep-frying
½ teaspoon ground turmeric
½ teaspoon ground coriander
½ teaspoon ground cumin
½ teaspoon chilli powder

Cut the chicken breasts into thin strips and toss in plain flour, shaking off the excess.

Fill a deep heavy-based pan one-third full of oil and heat to 180°C (350F), or until a cube of bread dropped into the oil browns in 15 seconds. Cook the goujons in batches for 3 minutes, or until golden. Drain on crumpled paper towels and keep warm.

Mix together the turmeric, coriander, cumin, chilli powder and 1 teaspoon salt. Toss the goujons in the mixture, shaking off the excess.

Makes about 30

Skordalia

(Greek garlic sauce)

500 g floury potatoes (see Notes)
5 cloves garlic, crushed
ground white pepper
3/4 cup (185 ml) olive oil
2 tablespoons white vinegar

Peel the potatoes and cut into 2 cm cubes. Bring a large saucepan of water to the boil, add the potato and cook for 10 minutes, or until very soft.

Drain the potato and mash until quite smooth. Stir in the garlic, 1 teaspoon salt and a pinch of ground white pepper. Gradually pour in the olive oil, mixing well with a wooden spoon. Add the vinegar and season to taste with additional salt and ground white pepper, if needed. Serve warm or cold with crusty bread or crackers, or with grilled meat, fish or chicken.

Makes 2 cups

Notes: Use King Edward, russet or pontiac potatoes.
Do not make skordalia with a food processor — the processing will turn the potato into a gluey mess.
Storage: Skordalia will keep in an airtight container for up to 2–3 days in the fridge. The potato will absorb the salt so check the seasoning before serving.

Deep-fried cheese ravioli

oil, for deep-frying
300 g fresh cheese ravioli (see Notes)

Fill a deep heavy based saucepan or deep-fryer one-third full of oil and heat to 180°C (350°F), or until a cube of bread dropped into the oil browns in 15 seconds. Cook the ravioli in batches until golden brown.

Remove from the oil and drain on crumpled paper towels. Sprinkle with salt and cracked black pepper, and serve hot.

Makes about 30

Notes: Ideal with green Mexican salsa (see page 86).
If you can't find fresh ravioli in sheets, individual pieces will work equally well.

Roasted vegetable pâté

500 g orange sweet potato, peeled
and cut into chunks
1 red or yellow capsicum (pepper),
cut into chunks
2 zucchini (courgette), sliced
350 g eggplant (aubergine), cut into
chunks
2 tomatoes, cut into chunks
8 spring onions, cut into lengths
1 tablespoon extra virgin olive oil
1 teaspoon sea salt
1 teaspoon grated lemon zest
2 tablespoons lemon juice

Preheat the oven to hot 220°C
(425°F/Gas 7). Place the vegetables
in a large baking dish, drizzle with oil,
sprinkle with sea salt and roast for
45 minutes, or until soft.

Transfer the vegetables to a food
processor, add the lemon zest and
the lemon juice. Blend until smooth.
Spoon into a serving dish and cool
to room temperature.

Makes 4 cups

Herbed parchment bread

1 cup (125 g) plain flour
2 tablespoons extra virgin olive oil
½ onion, chopped
¼ cup (15 g) fresh rosemary sprigs
¼ cup (15 g) fresh parsley
¼ cup (15 g) fresh mint leaves
2 teaspoons extra virgin olive oil, extra
sea salt

Preheat the oven to moderate 180°C (350°F/Gas 4). Process the flour and oil until the mixture resembles fine breadcrumbs. Transfer to a bowl.

Process the onion and herbs until finely chopped. Add 1 tablespoon of water and the extra oil and process until well combined. Add the herb mixture to the flour mixture and stir with a flat-bladed knife until it starts to come together. Add an extra tablespoon of water, if necessary. Press together and knead for 30 seconds.

Divide into 16 pieces and roll each piece between two sheets of non-stick baking paper as thinly as possible. Place on lightly greased baking trays in a single layer. Lightly brush with water and sprinkle with sea salt.

Bake each tray of breads for about 8 minutes, or until lightly browned and crisp to the touch. Transfer to wire racks to cool.

Makes 16

Tzatziki

2 Lebanese cucumbers
400 g Greek-style plain yoghurt
4 cloves garlic, crushed
3 tablespoons finely chopped fresh
    mint, plus extra to garnish
1 tablespoon lemon juice

Cut the cucumbers in half lengthways, scoop out the seeds and discard. Leave the skin on and coarsely grate the cucumber into a small colander. Sprinkle with salt and leave over a large bowl for 15 minutes to drain off any bitter juices.

Meanwhile, place the Greek-style yoghurt, crushed garlic, mint and lemon juice in a bowl, and stir until well combined.

Rinse the cucumber under cold water then, taking small handfuls, squeeze out any excess moisture. Combine the grated cucumber with the yoghurt mixture then season to taste with salt and freshly ground black pepper. Serve immediately or refrigerate until ready to serve, garnished with the extra mint.

Makes 2 cups

Note: Tzatziki is often served as a dip with flatbread or Turkish pide but is also suitable to serve as a sauce to accompany seafood and meat.
Storage: Tzatziki will keep in an airtight container in the refrigerator for 2–3 days.

Pesto bagel chips

4 three-day-old plain bagels
½ cup (125 g) ready-made pesto
1 cup (100 g) shredded Parmesan

Preheat the oven to warm 170°C (325°F/Gas 3). Slice each bagel into 6 thin rings.

Bake on a baking tray for 10 minutes. Brush with pesto and sprinkle with shredded Parmesan. Bake for a further 5 minutes, or until the chips are lightly golden.

Makes 24

Layered Mexican dip

450 g can refried beans
35 g sachet taco seasoning mix
300 g sour cream
1 quantity guacamole (see page 46)
200 g ready-made salsa sauce
  (medium heat)
1/2 cup (60 g) grated Cheddar
1 tablespoon chopped fresh coriander

Combine the beans and the
seasoning mix together in a bowl.

Spread the bean mixture over the
base of a serving plate, leaving
a border to place the corn chips.
Spread with the sour cream, then
guacamole, then salsa, layering
so you can see each separate layer.
Sprinkle with the cheese and
chopped coriander.

Makes 7 cups

Note: This makes a large portion
and is ideal for a large party. It can
be assembled on a large, flat plate
and surrounded by corn chips.

Parmesan puff straws

4 sheets ready-rolled puff pastry
50 g butter, melted
1²/₃ cups (165 g) finely grated
  Parmesan
1 egg, lightly beaten

Preheat the oven to moderately hot
200°C (400°F/Gas 6).

Lightly brush the pastry with the
butter, then sprinkle each sheet
with ¼ cup (25 g) of the cheese
and season with salt and pepper.
Fold each sheet in half, bringing the
top edge down towards you. Brush
the tops of each sheet with the egg.
Sprinkle each with 2 tablespoons of
extra grated Parmesan and season
with salt.

Using a very sharp knife, cut the
dough vertically into 1 cm wide strips.
Transfer each strip to a baking tray
lined with baking paper, spacing them
evenly. Hold each end of the pastry
and stretch and twist in opposite
directions. Bake in the oven for
10 minutes or until lightly browned.

Makes 80

Warm artichoke dip

2 x 400 g cans artichoke hearts,
    drained
1 cup (250 g) whole-egg mayonnaise
¾ cup (75 g) grated Parmesan
2 teaspoons onion flakes
2 tablespoons grated Parmesan,
    extra
ground paprika, to garnish

Preheat the oven to moderate 180°C (350°F/Gas 4). Squeeze the artichokes to remove any liquid. Chop finely and combine with the mayonnaise, Parmesan and onion flakes. Spread into a shallow 1 litre ovenproof dish.

Sprinkle with the extra Parmesan and paprika and bake for 15 minutes, or until lightly browned and heated through. Serve hot.

Makes 4 cups

Dipper ideas: Puff-pastry twists; crusty French bread.

Orange sweet potato wedges

1.3 kg orange sweet potato, peeled
  and sliced into 6 cm x 2 cm wedges
2 tablespoons olive oil
1 tablespoon fennel seeds
1 tablespoon coriander seeds
$1/2$ teaspoon cayenne pepper
1 teaspoon sea salt flakes

Preheat the oven to moderately hot 200°C (400°F/Gas 6).

Place the sweet potato in a large baking dish and toss with the oil.

In a mortar and pestle, pound together the fennel and coriander seeds until they are roughly crushed. Add to the orange sweet potato along with the cayenne and sea salt flakes. Toss well and bake for about 30 minutes, or until browned and crisp. Serve warm.

Serves 6–8

Parmesan, caper and basil spread

250 g light cream cheese, softened
½ cup (50 g) finely grated Parmesan
1½ tablespoons capers, rinsed, dried
   and roughly chopped
1½ tablespoons finely chopped fresh
   basil

Blend the cheeses in a bowl with a wooden spoon. Add the capers and basil. Season. Refrigerate for 1 hour to allow the flavours to develop.

Makes 1¼ cups

Dipper ideas: Two-seed crackers (page 33); herbed parchment bread (page 102).

Crispy bread fingers

2 tablespoons sweet chilli sauce
1 tablespoon peanut oil
1 loaf Turkish bread

Combine the sweet chilli sauce and peanut oil.

Cut the bread in half. Brush the top and bottom with the oil mixture.

Place on an oven tray and grill for 1–2 minutes, or until crispy and golden. Cut into 2 cm fingers.

Makes about 50

Spring onion flatbreads

2 teaspoons oil
185 g spring onions, thinly sliced
1 clove garlic, crushed
$\frac{1}{2}$ teaspoon grated fresh ginger
1$\frac{3}{4}$ cups (215 g) plain flour
1$\frac{1}{2}$ tablespoons chopped fresh
   coriander
oil, for shallow-frying

Heat the oil in a frying pan, and cook the spring onion, garlic and ginger for 2–3 minutes, or until soft.

Combine the flour and 1 teaspoon salt in a bowl. Stir in the spring onion mixture and the chopped coriander. Gradually stir in 1 cup (250 ml) boiling water, stopping when a loose dough forms. Knead the dough with floured hands for 1$\frac{1}{2}$–2 minutes, or until smooth. Cover with plastic wrap and rest for 30 minutes. Break off walnut-sized pieces of dough and roll them out into thin ovals.

Fill a large frying pan with 2 cm oil and heat over medium heat. When shimmering, cook the breads 2–3 at a time for 25–30 seconds each side, or until crisp and golden. Drain on paper towels and serve warm.

Makes 40

Dhal

1 cup (250 g) red lentils, rinsed
1/4 teaspoon ground turmeric
1 tablespoon oil
1 tablespoon cumin seeds
1/2 teaspoon brown mustard seeds
1 onion, finely chopped
1 tablespoon grated fresh ginger
2 long green chillies, seeded and
   finely chopped
1/3 cup (80 ml) lemon juice
2 tablespoons finely chopped fresh
   coriander leaves

Place the lentils in a saucepan with 3 cups (750 ml) cold water. Bring to the boil, then reduce the heat and stir in the turmeric. Simmer, covered, for 20 minutes, or until tender.

Meanwhile, heat the oil in a saucepan over medium heat, and cook the cumin and mustard seeds for 5–6 minutes, or until the seeds begin to pop. Add the onion, ginger and chilli and cook for 5 minutes, or until the onion is golden. Add the lentils and 1/2 cup (125 ml) water. Season with salt, reduce the heat and simmer for 10 minutes. Spoon into a bowl, stir in the lemon juice and garnish with coriander leaves.

Makes 3 cups

Cheese biscuits

1 cup (125 g) plain flour
2 tablespoons self-raising flour
1 teaspoon curry powder
125 g butter
½ cup (50 g) grated Parmesan
⅔ cup (85 g) grated Cheddar
20 g crumbled blue-vein cheese
1 tablespoon lemon juice
¼ cup (25 g) finely grated Parmesan,
  extra

Place the flours, curry powder and butter in a food processor. Process until the mixture resembles fine breadcrumbs.

Stir in the cheeses and the lemon juice. Bring the mixture together into a ball.

Roll into a 30 cm log. Wrap in plastic wrap and chill for 1 hour. Slice into 5 mm slices. Reshape if necessary. Preheat the oven to moderately hot 200°C (400°F/Gas 6).

Place on a baking paper-lined oven tray, allowing some room for spreading. Sprinkle the tops with Parmesan. Bake for 15 minutes, or until the biscuits are golden. Cool on the trays.

Makes about 40

Cold

Buckwheat blini with smoked salmon

7 g sachet dried yeast
pinch of sugar
1 cup (250 ml) warm milk
¾ cup (100 g) buckwheat flour
½ cup (60 g) plain flour
2 eggs, separated
20 g butter
⅓ cup (80 ml) oil
150 g crème fraîche
300 g smoked salmon, cut into
  2 cm strips
50 g salmon roe
fresh dill sprigs, to garnish

Place the yeast and sugar in a small bowl and gradually stir in the milk. Sift the flours into a large bowl and make a well in the centre. Add the egg yolks and warm milk mixture and whisk until combined and smooth. Cover and stand in a warm place for 45 minutes to prove.

Melt the butter, then stir into the proved dough and season. Place the egg whites in a clean dry bowl and beat with electric beaters until soft peaks form. Fold one third of the egg whites into the batter until just mixed. Gently fold in the remaining egg whites until just combined.

Heat 1 tablespoon of the oil in a large frying pan over medium heat. Drop ½ tablespoon of batter into the pan for each blini. Cook for 1 minute, or until bubbles form on the surface. Turn over and cook for 30 seconds, or until golden. Repeat to make about 40 blini, adding more oil as needed. Cool completely.

Spread 1 teaspoon of crème fraîche on each blini, then arrange a strip of smoked salmon over it. Spoon ¼ teaspoon of salmon roe on top. Garnish with a sprig of dill and serve.

Makes about 40

Cucumber cups with Thai beef salad

4 Lebanese cucumbers
oil, for pan-frying
250 g fillet steak
½ red onion, finely chopped
20 fresh mint leaves, finely chopped
1 tablespoon finely chopped fresh
  coriander leaves
1½ tablespoons fish sauce
1½ tablespoons lime juice
1 bird's eye chilli, seeded and finely
  chopped
1 teaspoon grated palm sugar or soft
  brown sugar
small coriander leaves, to garnish

Trim each end of the cucumbers but do not peel them. Cut each cucumber into 2 cm thick slices; you should get 24 pieces. Scoop out the centre of each slice with a melon baller, leaving a shell of flesh.

Heat a large frying pan over high heat and brush lightly with oil. Season the beef with salt and pepper, then place in the pan and cook for 1½–2 minutes each side, depending on the thickness (the beef needs to be rare). Set aside to rest for 5 minutes. Thinly slice the beef across the grain, then slice each piece into 5 mm wide strips and transfer to a bowl.

Add the onion, mint and coriander to the bowl and mix well. Combine the fish sauce, lime juice, chilli and sugar, stirring until the sugar has dissolved. Pour over the beef mixture and mix well. Fill each cucumber cup with the Thai beef salad and garnish with a whole coriander leaf.

Makes 24

Think ahead: The cups can be prepared a day early. To store them, directly cover the surface with plastic wrap to prevent them from drying out. Store in an airtight container. The meat can also be cooked a day early, but do not slice it until you are ready to assemble the salad.

Vegetable shapes with crème fraîche and fried leek

2 x 425 g long thin orange sweet
  potatoes, peeled
5 beetroots
½ cup (125 g) crème fraîche
1 clove garlic, crushed
¼ teaspoon finely grated lime zest
oil, for deep-frying
2 leeks, cut into thin 5 cm long strips

Put the orange sweet potato in one large saucepan of water and put the beetroots in another. Bring them to the boil over high heat and simmer, covered, for 30–40 minutes, or until tender, adding more boiling water if it starts to evaporate. Drain separately and set aside until cool enough to handle. Remove the skins from the beetroots. Trim the ends from the beetroots and sweet potatoes and cut both into 1 cm slices. Using a biscuit cutter, cut the thin slices into shapes. Leave to drain on paper towels.

Place the crème fraîche, garlic and lime zest in a bowl and mix together well. Refrigerate until ready to use.

Fill a deep heavy-based saucepan or deep-fryer one-third full of oil and heat to 190°C (375°F), or until a cube of bread dropped into the oil browns in 10 seconds. Cook the leek in four batches for 30 seconds, or until lightly golden and crisp. Drain on crumpled paper towels and season to taste with some salt.

To assemble, place a teaspoon of the crème fraîche mixture on top of each vegetable shape and top with some fried leek.

Makes 35

Prawn sushi cones

1½ cups (330 g) sushi rice or short-grain rice
2 tablespoons seasoned rice vinegar
1 avocado
1 small Lebanese cucumber
8 sheets nori, cut in half on the diagonal
1 teaspoon wasabi paste
80 g pickled ginger
16 cooked medium prawns, peeled and deveined
soy sauce, to serve

Place the rice in a sieve and rinse under cold running water. Set aside to drain for 1 hour. Place the drained rice in a large saucepan and add 1½ cups (375 ml) water. Cover and bring to the boil, then reduce the heat to very low and cook, tightly covered, for 15 minutes. Remove from the heat and leave the lid on for 10 minutes.

Transfer the rice to a large shallow bowl and drizzle with the vinegar. Fold the vinegar through the rice, tossing lightly with a large metal spoon or spatula to cool as you combine. Do not use a stirring action; it will make the rice mushy.

Quarter and peel the avocado and cut each quarter into four long wedges. Trim the ends of the cucumber, then cut lengthways into 16 strips.

Hold a sheet of nori shiny-side-down, flat in your hand. Place 2 tablespoons of rice on the left-hand side and spread out over half the nori sheet. Dab with a little wasabi and top with some pickled ginger. Place a strip each of avocado and cucumber on the rice and top with one prawn. Roll up the nori to form a cone, enclosing the smaller end. Repeat, using all the ingredients. Serve with soy sauce.

Makes 16

Cold

Cherry tomato and bocconcini tartlets

2 cups (250 g) plain flour
125 g chilled butter, chopped
1 egg

Filling
300 g cherry tomatoes, quartered
2 tablespoons olive oil
1 clove garlic, crushed
200 g bocconcini, quartered
80 g chopped Kalamata olives
1 tablespoon extra virgin olive oil
1 tablespoon torn fresh basil
oil, for deep-frying
30 small fresh basil leaves

Preheat the oven to moderately hot 200°C (400°F/Gas 6). Grease 30 mini muffin holes. Sift the flour and rub the butter in with your fingertips until the mixture resembles fine breadcrumbs. Make a well, add the egg and mix with a flat-bladed knife, using a cutting action, until it gathers in beads. Add a little cold water if necessary. Press the dough into a ball, wrap in plastic wrap and chill for 30 minutes.

Roll out the dough between two sheets of baking paper to 2 mm thick and cut 30 rounds with a 6 cm cutter. Press a round into each muffin hole. Prick each base with a fork and bake for 6 minutes, or until dry and golden. If they puff up, use a clean tea towel to press back. Cool.

To make the filling, preheat the oven to moderately hot 200°C (400°F/ Gas 6). Combine the tomatoes, olive oil and garlic in a roasting tin and bake for 15 minutes, or until golden. Cool, add the bocconcini, olives, extra virgin olive oil and basil, season, and toss. Fill a saucepan one-third full of oil and heat to 180°C (350°F), or until a cube of bread browns in 15 seconds. Deep-fry the basil in batches for 30 seconds, or until crisp. Drain. Spoon the vegetable mixture into the pastry cases and top with a basil leaf.

Makes 30

Dolmades

200 g packet vine leaves in brine
1 cup (250 g) medium-grain rice
1 small onion, finely chopped
1 tablespoon olive oil
50 g pine nuts, toasted
2 tablespoons currants
2 tablespoons chopped fresh dill
2 tablespoons finely chopped
fresh mint
2 tablespoons finely chopped fresh
flat-leaf parsley
1/3 cup (80 ml) olive oil, extra
2 tablespoons lemon juice
2 cups (500 ml) chicken or vegetable
stock

Cover the vine leaves with cold water and soak for 15 minutes. Pat dry and cut off any stems. Reserve 5–6 leaves; discard any with holes. Meanwhile, pour boiling water over the rice and soak for 10 minutes, then drain.

Place the rice, onion, oil, pine nuts, currants, herbs and salt and pepper in a large bowl, and mix well.

Lay some leaves vein-side-down on a flat surface. Place 1/2 tablespoon of filling in the middle of each leaf, fold the stalk end over the filling, then the left and right sides into the middle, and finally roll firmly towards the tip. The dolmade should resemble a small cigar. Repeat to make 48 dolmades.

Line the base of a large, heavy-based saucepan or flameproof casserole dish with the reserved leaves. Drizzle with 1 tablespoon of the extra oil. Put the dolmades in the pan, packing them tightly in one layer. Pour the remaining oil and lemon juice over them.

Pour the stock over the dolmades and cover with an inverted plate to stop them moving while cooking. Bring to the boil, then reduce the heat and simmer gently, covered, for 45 minutes. Remove with a slotted spoon. Serve warm or cold.

Makes 48

Oysters with lemon herb dressing

24 fresh oysters (see Notes)
1 tablespoon chopped fresh dill
1 clove garlic, crushed
1 tablespoon finely chopped fresh
  flat-leaf parsley
2 teaspoons finely chopped fresh
  chives
2 tablespoons lemon juice
1/4 cup (60 ml) extra virgin olive oil
chive bows, to garnish
brown bread, cubed, to garnish

Remove the oysters from the shells and pat dry. Wash the shells, replace the oysters and cover with a damp cloth in the fridge.

Place the dill, garlic, parsley, chives, lemon juice and oil in a bowl and season to taste with salt and cracked black pepper. Mix together well, then drizzle a little of the dressing over each oyster.

Garnish with chive bows and serve with tiny cubes of brown bread.

Makes 24

Notes: Oysters are sold freshly shucked on the half shell, or alive and unshucked. When buying fresh shucked oysters, look for a plump, moist oyster. The flesh should be creamy with a clear liquid (oyster liquor) surrounding it. Oysters should smell like the fresh sea and have no traces of shell particles.
If you prefer to shuck the oysters yourself, look for tightly closed, unbroken shells.
Oysters are often served on a bed of rock salt or crushed ice to help them remain stable and upright, and to keep them cool in summer.

Mandarin and duck rice paper rolls

1 whole Chinese roast duck
24 small Vietnamese rice paper
    wrappers
3 mandarins, peeled and segmented
1 cup (20 g) fresh mint
60 g fresh chives, cut into 3–4 cm
    lengths
2 tablespoons hoisin sauce
2 tablespoons fresh mandarin juice

Remove the flesh and skin from the duck and shred into 1 cm x 3 cm pieces.

Working with one wrapper at a time, briefly soak each wrapper in cold water until softened, then place on a dry tea towel. Arrange 2–3 pieces of duck at the end of the wrapper closest to you. Top with 2 segments of mandarin, 3 mint leaves and several lengths of chives. Fold the end closest to you over the filling, fold in the sides and firmly roll up the rice paper to form a small spring roll.

Combine the hoisin sauce and mandarin juice in a bowl and serve as a dipping sauce with the rice paper rolls. These are best served immediately as the rolls will start to dry out if left for too long.

Makes 24

Rolled omelette with ocean trout caviar

4 eggs
1/3 cup (80 ml) thick (double) cream
4 tablespoons finely chopped fresh
  chives
1 tablespoon olive oil
40 g butter, melted
3 slices white bread
1/4 cup (60 g) sour cream
100 g ocean trout caviar or salmon
  roe
chopped fresh chives, to garnish

Whisk together one egg, 1 tablespoon of the cream and 1 tablespoon of the chopped chives, and season with salt and cracked black pepper. Pour into a 25 cm lightly greased non-stick frying pan and cook over medium heat on one side for 3 minutes, or until just set; the omelettes will be difficult to roll if cooked for too long. Turn out onto a sheet of baking paper. Repeat with the remaining eggs and cream until you have four omelettes.

Tightly roll one omelette into a neat roll, then take another omelette and wrap it around the first. Repeat with the remaining omelettes so that you have two rolls. Wrap separately in plastic wrap and refrigerate for 1 hour.

Meanwhile preheat the oven to moderate 180°C (350°F/Gas 4). Combine the oil and butter. Using a 3 cm cutter, cut 24 rounds from the bread and brush with the butter and oil mixture. Place on a baking tray and bake for 20–30 minutes, or until crisp and golden. Allow to cool.

Cut each of the cooled omelette rolls into 12 rounds. Spread 1/2 teaspoon of the sour cream onto each croûton, and sit a round of omelette on top. Top with a teaspoon of salmon roe and garnish with chopped chives.

Makes 24

Cold

Chicken liver parfait

35 g butter
2 French shallots, peeled and sliced
500 g chicken livers, trimmed
¼ cup (60 ml) thick cream
1 tablespoon cognac or brandy
48 Melba toasts
8 cornichons (baby gherkins), thinly
    sliced on the diagonal

Heat a large frying pan over medium heat. Melt the butter, then add the shallots to the pan and cook, stirring, for 4–5 minutes, or until they are soft and transparent. Use a slotted spoon to transfer them to a food processor.

In the same pan, add the chicken livers and cook in batches over high heat, stirring, for 4–5 minutes, or until seared on the outside but still pink and quite soft on the inside. Add to the food processor along with 2 tablespoons of the pan juices, the cream, cognac and some salt and pepper. Blend for 4–5 minutes, or until quite smooth. Push through a fine sieve to remove any remaining lumps. Transfer to a bowl or serving dish, put plastic wrap directly on the surface of the mixture and refrigerate for at least 4 hours, or until cold.

To serve, spoon a heaped teaspoon of parfait onto each Melba toast and top with a slice of cornichon. Alternatively, leave the parfait in the serving dish, supply a small knife and allow guests to help themselves.

Makes 48

Think ahead: The parfait can be made up to 3 days in advance and stored in the fridge in an airtight container. Assemble no more than 30 minutes before serving.

Quail eggs with spiced salts

2 teaspoons cumin seeds
48 quail eggs
½ cup (125 g) good-quality table salt
1½ teaspoons Chinese five-spice
  powder
3 teaspoons celery salt

Toast the cumin seeds in a dry frying pan over low heat for 1–2 minutes, or until fragrant. Cool slightly, then grind until finely crushed into a powder.

Place half the eggs in a large saucepan of water, bring to the boil and cook for 1½ minutes for medium-hard boiled eggs. Remove from the pan and rinse under cold water to cool. Repeat with the remaining eggs. Peel when cold — this is easiest done under gently running cold water.

Divide the table salt among three small bowls and add the Chinese five-spice powder to one, the celery salt to another and the ground cumin to the third. Mix the flavourings into the salt in each bowl.

To serve, pile the eggs into a large bowl and serve each of the salts in a small bowl. Invite your guests to dip their egg into the flavoured salt of their choice.

Makes 48

Think ahead: The eggs can be prepared the day before they are to be served and the spiced salts can be made up to 2 weeks earlier and stored in airtight containers.

Asparagus and prosciutto bundles with hollandaise

24 spears fresh asparagus, trimmed
8 slices prosciutto, cut into thirds
  lengthways

Hollandaise
175 g butter
4 egg yolks
1 tablespoon lemon juice
ground white pepper

Blanch the asparagus in boiling salted water for 2 minutes, then drain and refresh in cold water. Pat dry, then cut the spears in half. Lay the bottom half of each spear next to its tip, then secure together by wrapping a piece of prosciutto around them.

To make the hollandaise, melt the butter in a small saucepan. Skim any froth off the top. Cool the butter a little. Combine the egg yolks and 2 tablespoons of water in a small heatproof bowl placed over a saucepan of simmering water, making sure the base of the bowl does not touch the water. Using a wire whisk, beat for about 3–4 minutes, or until the mixture is thick and foamy. Make sure the bowl does not get too hot or you will end up with scrambled eggs. Add the butter slowly, a little at a time at first, whisking well between each addition. Keep adding the butter in a thin stream, whisking continuously, until all the butter has been used. Try to avoid using the milky whey in the bottom of the pan, but don't worry if a little gets in. Stir in the lemon juice and season with salt and white pepper. Place in a bowl and serve warm with the asparagus.

Makes 24 bundles

Vegetable frittata with hummus and black olives

2 large red capsicums (peppers)
600 g orange sweet potato, cut into
   1 cm slices
1/4 cup (60 ml) olive oil
2 leeks, finely sliced
2 cloves garlic, crushed
250 g zucchini (courgette), thinly
   sliced
500 g eggplant (aubergine), cut into
   1 cm slices
8 eggs, lightly beaten
2 tablespoons finely chopped fresh
   basil
1 1/4 cups (125 g) grated Parmesan
200 g ready-made hummus
black olives, pitted and halved,
   to garnish

Cut the capsicums into large pieces, removing the seeds and membrane. Place, skin-side-up, under a hot grill until the skin blackens and blisters. Cool in a plastic bag, then peel.

Cook the sweet potato in a saucepan of boiling water for 4–5 minutes, or until just tender. Drain.

Heat 1 tablespoon of the oil in a deep 23 cm frying pan over medium heat. Stir in the leek and garlic for 1 minute, or until soft. Add the zucchini and cook for 2 minutes then remove.

Heat the remaining oil in the same pan and cook the eggplant in batches for 2 minutes each side, or until golden. Line the base of the pan with half the eggplant and spread with the leek mixture. Cover with the roasted capsicum, then with the remaining eggplant and finally, the sweet potato.

Place the eggs, basil, Parmesan and pepper in a jug and mix well. Pour over the vegetables. Cook over low heat for 15 minutes, or until almost cooked. Place the pan under a hot grill for 2–3 minutes, or until golden and cooked. Cool before inverting onto a board. Trim the edges and cut into 30 squares. Top each square with a dollop of hummus and half an olive.

Makes 30 pieces

Smoked trout sandwiches

24 thin slices brown bread
softened cream cheese, to spread
1 large telegraph cucumber, cut into
  wafer-thin slices
400 g good-quality smoked trout
2 tablespoons roughly chopped
  fresh dill
lemon wedges, to garnish

Spread the bread with cream cheese. Arrange a single layer of cucumber on half the bread slices. Layer the trout on top of the cucumber, then place the other bread slices on top. Cut off the crusts, then slice each sandwich into four triangles.

Place the sandwiches long-edge-down on a platter to form a pyramid. Brush one side of the pyramid with softened cream cheese, then sprinkle with dill. Garnish with lemon.

Makes 48

Mexican bites

740 g can kidney beans, drained
1 teaspoon ground cumin
2 tablespoons olive oil
1/4 teaspoon cayenne pepper
1 avocado
1 small clove garlic, crushed
2 tablespoons sour cream
2 tablespoons lime juice
1 vine-ripened tomato, seeded
   and finely chopped
2 tablespoons finely chopped fresh
   coriander
250 g packet round tortilla chips

To make the refried beans, put the kidney beans in a bowl and mash well with a potato masher, then add the cumin. Heat 1 1/2 tablespoons of oil in a large non-stick frying pan and add the cayenne pepper and mashed kidney beans. Cook over medium–high heat for 2–3 minutes, stirring constantly. Allow to cool, then refrigerate for about 30 minutes, or until cold.

Scoop the avocado flesh into a food processor and add the garlic, sour cream and 1 tablespoon of the lime juice. Process for a few minutes until it is a thick creamy paste, then add salt to taste. Refrigerate.

To make the salsa, mix together the tomato, coriander and the remaining olive oil and lime juice in a bowl. Refrigerate until needed.

To assemble, lay out 36 round tortilla chips. Put a heaped teaspoon of refried beans in the centre of each chip, add a teaspoon of the avocado cream and lastly half a teaspoon of tomato salsa.

Makes 36

Think ahead: The bean purée can be made 3 days in advance. Make the salsa up to 2 hours beforehand. Assemble just before serving.

Vietnamese prawn rolls

²/₃ cup (170 ml) lime juice
2 teaspoons grated lime zest
¹/₃ cup (80 ml) sweet chilli sauce
2 teaspoons fish sauce
2 teaspoons grated palm sugar
  or soft brown sugar
12 x 15 cm rice paper wrappers
12 cooked medium prawns, peeled
  and halved lengthways
1 small carrot, cut into 5 cm long
  julienne strips
1 small Lebanese cucumber, cut
  into 5 cm batons
¹/₂ avocado, sliced
3 tablespoons fresh coriander leaves
2 tablespoons torn fresh Vietnamese
  mint
5 spring onions, thinly sliced on the
  diagonal

Combine the lime juice and zest, sweet chilli sauce, fish sauce and sugar in a small bowl.

Working with one rice paper wrapper at a time, dip a wrapper in a bowl of warm water for 10 seconds to soften, then lay out on a flat surface. Place 2 prawn halves and a little of each remaining ingredient at one end of the wrapper, then drizzle with 1 teaspoon of the sauce. Fold in the sides and roll up tightly. Serve with the remaining sauce for dipping.

Makes 12

Asian-flavoured crab tartlets

2 cups (250 g) plain flour
125 g chilled butter, chopped
1 egg

Filling
¼ cup (60 ml) lime juice
1 tablespoon fish sauce
1 tablespoon grated palm sugar or
  soft brown sugar
300 g fresh crab meat, shredded and
  well drained
2 tablespoons chopped fresh
  coriander leaves
1 tablespoon chopped fresh
  Vietnamese mint
1 small fresh red chilli, finely chopped
2 kaffir lime leaves, finely shredded

Preheat the oven to moderately hot 200°C (400°F/Gas 6). Lightly grease 30 mini muffin holes. Sift the flour into a bowl and rub the butter in with your fingertips until the mixture resembles fine breadcrumbs. Make a well in the centre, add the egg and mix with a flat-bladed knife, using a cutting action until it comes together in beads. If the dough seems too dry, add a little cold water. Press the dough into a ball on a lightly floured surface, then wrap it in plastic wrap and refrigerate for 30 minutes.

Roll out the dough between two sheets of baking paper to 2 mm thick and cut out 30 rounds with a 6 cm cutter. Press a round into each muffin hole. Prick the bases with a fork and bake for 6–8 minutes, or until golden. If they puff up, use a clean tea towel to press out any air pockets. Cool.

Combine the lime juice, fish sauce and sugar in a bowl and stir until the sugar is dissolved. Mix in the rest of the ingredients, then spoon into the prepared pastry cases and serve.

Makes 30

Plan ahead: The pastry cases can be made 2–3 days ahead and kept in an airtight container. If they go soft, crisp them in a warm (170°C/325°F/ Gas 3) oven for 5 minutes.

Vietnamese rice paper rolls

Nuoc cham dipping sauce
3/4 cup (185 ml) fish sauce
1/4 cup (60 ml) lime juice
2 tablespoons grated palm sugar or
  soft brown sugar
2 bird's eye chillies, seeded
  and finely chopped

150 g dried rice vermicelli
48 round 15 cm rice paper wrappers
48 cooked king prawns, peeled,
  deveined and halved lengthways
150 g bean sprouts
3 cups (60 g) fresh mint
2 cups (60 g) fresh coriander leaves

To make the dipping sauce, combine all the ingredients and 1/2 cup (125 ml) water and stir until the sugar dissolves. Transfer to two small serving dishes and set aside.

Place the noodles in a heatproof bowl, cover with boiling water and soak for 10 minutes, then drain.

Assemble the rolls one at a time. Dip a rice paper wrapper in a bowl of warm water for 30 seconds, or until it softens. Place the wrapper on a work surface and put 2 prawn halves on the bottom third of the wrapper. Top with a few noodles, bean sprouts, 3 mint leaves and 6 coriander leaves, in that order. Ensure that the filling is neat and compact, then turn up the bottom of the wrapper to cover the filling. Holding the filling in place, fold in the two sides, then roll up.

Arrange on a platter, folded-side-down. Cover with a damp tea towel or plastic wrap until ready to serve. Serve with the dipping sauce.

Makes 48

Think ahead: You can make the rolls up to 8 hours beforehand, but make sure you cover them well or they will dry out rapidly. The sauce can be made a day early.

Smoked fish pâté
with bruschetta

2 x 400 g smoked rainbow trout fillets
2–3 tablespoons lemon or lime juice
125 g cream cheese, softened
200 g butter, melted
sprigs of fresh herbs such as dill,
    fennel or flat-leaf parsley, to garnish
lemon slices, to garnish

Bruschetta
1 bread stick, sliced diagonally into
    24 thin slices
1/3 cup (80 ml) olive oil
3 cloves garlic

Remove the skin and bones from the fish and roughly flake the flesh. Process the flesh in a blender or food processor with the juice, cream cheese and melted butter until the mixture is quite smooth. Season to taste with ground black pepper.

Spoon into a 2-cup ramekin and refrigerate overnight, or until the mixture has firmed. Keep refrigerated until ready to serve. Garnish with sprigs of fresh herbs and lemon slices.

For the bruschetta, preheat the oven to moderately hot 200°C (400°F/ Gas 6). Brush both sides of the bread slices lightly with oil, then spread on a baking tray and bake for about 10–15 minutes, or until crisp and golden, turning once. Remove from the oven and rub all over one side of each slice with a garlic clove, using a clove for every 8 slices. Serve with the pâté.

Makes 2 cups.

Soy bean terrine

1 cup (200 g) dried soy beans
1 tablespoon soy bean oil
1 onion, finely chopped
1 zucchini (courgette), grated
1/4 cup (7 g) finely chopped fresh
   flat-leaf parsley
1 teaspoon cayenne pepper
3 eggs, lightly beaten
1/3 cup (90 g) sour cream
1/4 cup (60 ml) lemon juice
2 cups (250 g) grated Cheddar
1/2 cup (50 g) grated Parmesan
tomato relish, to serve

Soak the soy beans in a bowl with plenty of cold water for at least 8 hours, or preferably overnight. Drain well. Place the soy beans in a large saucepan and add enough water to cover the beans. Bring to the boil, then simmer for 1 hour 30 minutes, or until tender. Drain.

Preheat the oven to moderately hot 190°C (375°F/Gas 5). Lightly grease a 22 x 12 cm loaf tin and line the base and sides with baking paper. Blend the beans in a food processor until crumbly.

Heat the oil in a large frying pan. Add the onion and zucchini and cook over medium heat for 5 minutes, or until golden. Transfer to a bowl and allow to cool.

Add the parsley, cayenne pepper, egg, sour cream, lemon juice, cheeses and soy beans and mix together. Spoon the mixture into the prepared tin and press down to flatten the top. Bake for 45 minutes, or until firm. Cool completely in the tin, then carefully invert on a platter. Serve sliced, topped with some tomato relish and garnished with cherry tomatoes and thyme.

Serves 6–8

Corn muffins

2½ cups (310 g/10 oz) self-raising
    flour
½ cup (75 g/2½ oz) cornmeal
1 cup (250 ml/8 fl oz) milk
125 g (4 oz) butter, melted
2 eggs, lightly beaten
130 g (4½ oz) can corn kernels,
    drained
2 spring onions, finely chopped
½ cup (60 g/2 oz) grated Cheddar

Preheat the oven to hot 210°C
(415°F/Gas 6–7). Grease two trays of
six ½-cup (125 ml/4 fl oz) muffin holes
with butter. Sift the flour and cornmeal
into a large bowl and make a well in
the centre.

Whisk together the milk, butter, eggs,
corn, spring onion, Cheddar and salt
and pepper in a separate bowl and
pour into the well. Fold gently with a
metal spoon until all the ingredients
are just combined. Do not overmix—
the mixture should still be very lumpy.

Spoon the mixture into the tin and
bake for 20–25 minutes, or until lightly
golden. Leave for 5 minutes before
removing from the tin. Serve split in
half spread with butter or cream
cheese. Delicious warm or at room
temperature.

Makes 12

Variation: Try adding 2 tablespoons
chopped chives, ¼ cup (40 g)
chopped, drained sun-dried tomato
or capsicum in oil, 2 finely chopped
rashers of bacon, 2 finely chopped
red chillies or ½ finely chopped red
or green capsicum into the mixture
with the milk and Cheddar. Another
delicious variation is to sprinkle
sesame or sunflower seeds over
the muffins just before baking.

Bloody Mary oyster shots

⅓ cup (80 ml) vodka
½ cup (125 ml) tomato juice
1 tablespoon lemon juice
dash of Worcestershire sauce
2 drops of Tabasco sauce
pinch of celery salt
12 oysters
1 cucumber, peeled, seeded and
   finely julienned

Combine the vodka, tomato juice, lemon juice, Worcestershire sauce, Tabasco and celery salt in a jug. Mix well, then refrigerate for 30 minutes, or until chilled.

Just before serving, fill each shot glass about two-thirds full. Drop an oyster in each glass, then top with a teaspoon of julienned cucumber. For the final touch, crack some black pepper over the top of each shot glass, then serve.

Serves 12

Note: It is better to use oysters fresh from the shell rather than from a jar because they have a much better, fresher taste.
Think ahead: The tomato mixture can be made a day ahead of time and kept in the fridge. Stir before serving.
Variation: If you think your guests are game enough for some fire in their evening, make chilled sake shots.
Fill each glass two-thirds full of sake, add an oyster, then garnish with the julienned cucumber.

Smoked salmon bread baskets

250 g smoked salmon
1 loaf white sliced bread
1/4 cup (60 ml) olive oil
1/3 cup (90 g) whole-egg mayonnaise
2 teaspoons extra virgin olive oil
1 teaspoon white wine vinegar
1 teaspoon finely chopped fresh dill
3 teaspoons horseradish cream
3 tablespoons salmon roe
fresh dill sprigs, to garnish

Preheat the oven to moderate 180°C (350°F/Gas 4). Cut the salmon into 2 cm wide strips. Flatten the bread to 1 mm with a rolling pin, then cut out 24 rounds with a 7 cm cutter. Brush both sides of the rounds with oil and push into the holes of two 12-hole flat-based patty tins. Bake for 10 minutes, or until crisp. Cool.

Stir the mayonnaise in a bowl with the extra virgin olive oil, vinegar, dill and horseradish until combined.

Arrange folds of salmon in each cooled bread case and top each with 1 teaspoon of mayonnaise mixture. Spoon 1/2 teaspoon of salmon roe on top of each, garnish with dill and serve.

Makes 24

Note: The bread cases can be made a day in advance. When completely cold, store in an airtight container. If they soften, you can crisp them on a baking tray in a moderate 180°C (350°F/Gas 4) oven for 5 minutes. Cool before filling.

Herbed pikelets with pear and blue cheese topping

1 cup (125 g) self-raising flour
2 eggs, lightly beaten
½ cup (125 ml) milk
2 tablespoons finely chopped fresh
  parsley
2 teaspoons finely chopped fresh
  sage

Pear and blue cheese topping
100 g Blue Castello or other creamy
  blue cheese
75 g cream cheese
2 teaspoons brandy
1 large ripe green-skinned pear
¼ cup (30 g) toasted walnuts, finely
  chopped
½ lemon
30 g chives, cut into 3–4 cm lengths

Sift the flour into a bowl and make a well in the centre. Gradually add the combined eggs and milk, mixing the flour in slowly. When the flour is incorporated, add the parsley and sage and season well. Whisk until a smooth batter forms.

Heat a large non-stick frying pan over medium heat and spray with cooking oil spray. Drop heaped teaspoons of batter into the pan and flatten them to give 5 cm circles. Cook until bubbles appear in the surface of the pikelet, then turn and brown the other side. Lift out to cool on a wire rack.

To make the topping, beat the cheeses and brandy together until smooth. Season with pepper. Cut the pear in half and peel and core one half, then dice it into 5 mm pieces, leaving the other half untouched. Stir the diced pear and walnuts into the cheese mixture. Core the other half of the pear but do not peel it. Thinly slice the pear lengthways. Cut each slice into 2 cm triangles with green skin on one side. Squeeze some lemon juice over the cut surfaces to prevent discoloration.

Spread 1 teaspoon of topping on each pikelet. Arrange three pear triangles on top and garnish with chives.

Makes 36

Mini frittatas

1 kg orange sweet potato
1 tablespoon oil
30 g butter
4 leeks, white part only, finely sliced
2 cloves garlic, crushed
250 g feta cheese, crumbled
8 eggs
1/2 cup (125 ml) cream

Preheat the oven to moderate 180°C (350°F/Gas 4). Grease or brush a tray of twelve 1-cup (125 ml) muffin holes with oil or melted butter. Cut small rounds of baking paper and place into the base of each hole. Cut the sweet potato into small cubes and boil, steam or microwave until tender. Drain well and set aside.

Heat the oil and butter in a frying pan and cook the leek for 10 minutes, stirring occasionally, or until very soft and lightly golden. Add the garlic and cook for a further 1 minute. Cool, then stir in the feta and sweet potato. Divide the mixture evenly among the muffin holes.

Whisk the eggs and cream together and season with salt and cracked black pepper. Pour the egg mixture into each hole until three-quarters filled, then press the vegetables down gently. Bake for 25–30 minutes, or until golden and set. Leave in the tins for 5 minutes, then ease out with a knife and cool on a wire rack.

Makes 12

Thai beef salad rice paper rolls

Dipping sauce
¼ cup (60 ml) Japanese soy sauce
1 tablespoon rice vinegar
1 teaspoon sesame oil
1 tablespoon mirin
2 teaspoons finely julienned fresh
  ginger

⅓ cup (80 ml) kecap manis
⅓ cup (80 ml) lime juice
1 tablespoon sesame oil
2 small red chillies, finely chopped
300 g piece beef eye fillet
1 stem lemon grass, white part only,
  finely chopped
¼ cup (60 ml) lime juice, extra
3 tablespoons finely chopped fresh
  mint
3 tablespoons finely chopped fresh
  coriander leaves
1½ tablespoons fish sauce
16 square (16.5 cm) rice paper
  wrappers

To make the dipping sauce, place the Japanese soy sauce, rice vinegar, sesame oil, mirin and ginger in a small bowl and mix together well.

Mix the kecap manis, lime juice, sesame oil and half the chilli in a large bowl. Add the beef and toss well to ensure all the beef is coated. Cover with plastic wrap and refrigerate for 2 hours.

Heat a barbecue or chargrill plate over high heat and cook the beef for 2–3 minutes each side, or until cooked to your liking. Cool, then slice into thin strips, against the grain.

Combine the beef with the lemon grass, extra lime juice, chopped mint, coriander, fish sauce and remaining chilli, then toss well.

Dip one rice paper wrapper at a time in warm water for a few seconds until softened. Drain, then place on a flat surface. Place a tablespoon of the mixture in the centre of the rice paper wrapper and roll up, tucking in the edges. Repeat with the remaining ingredients to make 16 rolls in total. Serve with the dipping sauce.

Makes 16

Maki zushi

1 1/4 cups (275 g) sushi rice
50 ml rice vinegar
1 tablespoon sugar
1/2 tablespoon mirin

250 g sashimi tuna
1 small Lebanese cucumber
1/2 avocado
8 sheets nori
3 teaspoons wasabi paste

Rinse the rice under running water until the water runs clear, then drain thoroughly. Place in a large saucepan with 1 1/2 cups (375 ml) water and simmer for 20–25 minutes, or until tender. Cover with a clean tea towel and leave for 15 minutes.

Combine the vinegar, sugar, mirin, and 1 teaspoon salt, and stir until the sugar dissolves. Spread the rice over a non-metallic tray and pour the dressing on top. Mix with a spatula, gently separating the grains of rice. Allow to cool to body temperature.

Cut the tuna, cucumber and avocado into thin strips. Place a sheet of nori on a bamboo mat (available at Asian grocery stores), shiny-side-down, with a short end towards you. Spread the rice 1 cm thick over the nori, leaving a 1 cm border. Make a shallow groove down the centre of the rice towards the short end closest to you. Spread some wasabi along the groove. Place a selection of strips of your filling ingredients on top of the wasabi. Lift the edge of the bamboo mat and roll the sushi, starting from the edge nearest to you. When you've finished rolling, press the mat to make either a round or square roll. Wet a sharp knife, trim the ends and cut the roll into six pieces.

Makes 48

Wild mushroom pâté on Melba toasts

20 g dried wild mixed forest
    mushrooms (e.g. cep, chanterelles,
    black chanterelles)
50 g butter
375 g flat mushrooms, sliced
1 garlic clove, crushed
2 tablespoons brandy
¼ cup (60 ml) thick cream
1 teaspoon fresh thyme
¼ teaspoon juniper berries, ground
100 g ready-made mini Melba toasts
crème fraîche, to serve
30 fresh flat-leaf parsley leaves

Soak the dried mushrooms in a bowl with 1 cup (250 ml) hot (not boiling) water for 2 hours, or until soft. Drain, reserving 2 tablespoons of the soaking liquid. Discard any pieces of mushroom that are still tough and woody after soaking.

Melt the butter in a large frying pan over medium heat, then add the flat mushrooms and sauté for 5 minutes. Add the garlic and cook for 1 minute, then add the dried mushrooms and reserved soaking liquid and cook for another 5–8 minutes, stirring regularly. Pour in the brandy and cook for 2 minutes, or until evaporated. Remove from the heat and allow to cool for 10 minutes.

Transfer the cooled mushroom mixture to a food processor with the cream, thyme, ground juniper berries and ½ teaspoon each of salt and cracked black pepper and blend for 4–5 minutes, or until finely chopped.

Spoon the pâté into a bowl and refrigerate, covered, for at least 3 hours, or until chilled. Dollop a teaspoon of pâté on each toast and top each toast with ½ teaspoon crème fraîche and a fresh parsley leaf.

Makes 30

Hot

Steamed prawn nori rolls

500 g peeled raw prawns, deveined
1½ tablespoons fish sauce
1 tablespoon sake
2 tablespoons chopped fresh
   coriander
1 large fresh kaffir lime leaf, finely
   shredded
1 tablespoon lime juice
2 teaspoons sweet chilli sauce
1 egg white, lightly beaten
5 sheets nori

Dipping sauce
¼ cup (60 ml) sake
¼ cup (60 ml) soy sauce
1 tablespoon mirin
1 tablespoon lime juice

Process the prawns in a food processor or blender with the fish sauce, sake, coriander, kaffir lime leaf, lime juice and sweet chilli sauce, until smooth. Add the egg white and pulse for a few seconds to just combine.

Lay the nori sheets on a flat surface and spread some prawn mixture over each sheet, leaving a 2 cm border at one end. Roll up tightly, cover and refrigerate for 1 hour to firm. Using a very sharp knife, trim the ends, then cut into 2 cm lengths.

Place the rolls in a lined bamboo steamer. Cover the steamer and place it over a wok of simmering water, making sure it doesn't touch the water. Steam the rolls for about 5 minutes, or until heated thoroughly.

For the dipping sauce, thoroughly mix all the ingredients together in a small bowl. Serve with the nori rolls.

Makes 25

Chicken san choy bau

1½ tablespoons vegetable oil
¼ teaspoon sesame oil
3 cloves garlic, crushed
3 teaspoons grated fresh ginger
6 spring onions, thinly sliced
500 g chicken mince
100 g drained water chestnuts,
  finely chopped
100 g drained bamboo shoots,
  finely chopped
¼ cup (60 ml) oyster sauce
2 teaspoons soy sauce
¼ cup (60 ml) sherry
1 teaspoon sugar
4 small witlof (chicory) heads, bases
  trimmed
oyster sauce, to serve

Heat the oils in a wok or large frying pan, add the garlic, ginger and half the spring onion, and stir-fry over high heat for 1 minute. Add the mince and continue cooking for 3–4 minutes, or until just cooked, breaking up any lumps with a fork.

Add the water chestnuts, bamboo shoots, oyster and soy sauces, sherry, sugar and the remaining spring onion. Cook for 2–3 minutes, or until the liquid thickens a little.

Allow the mixture to cool slightly before dividing among the witlof leaves; you will need about 2 heaped teaspoons per leaf. Drizzle with oyster sauce and serve immediately.

Makes about 36

Think ahead: The filling can be made up to 2 days in advance and reheated just before assembling.
Variations: Pork mince is another popular choice for san choy bau: you can either swap it directly for the chicken mince or use half of each and mix them together.
There are also several types of leaves that work well for cupping the filling. Try the small leaves from a cos or iceberg lettuce or, for a more sophisticated option, try betel leaves, available from Indian food suppliers.

Capsicum muffins with tapenade and mascarpone

1 red capsicum (pepper), cut into
  large, flattish pieces
2 cups (250 g) plain flour
3 teaspoons baking powder
3/4 cup (75 g) grated Parmesan
1/2 cup (125 ml) milk
2 eggs, lightly beaten
1/4 cup (60 ml) olive oil
1 1/2 tablespoons olive oil, extra
24 fresh basil leaves
1/3 cup (75 g) mascarpone

Tapenade
1/2 cup (80 g) pitted Kalamata olives
1 clove garlic, chopped
2 anchovies (optional)
2 teaspoons drained capers
2 tablespoons olive oil
2 teaspoons lemon juice

Cook the capsicum, skin-side-up, under a hot grill until the skin blisters. Allow to cool in a plastic bag. Peel the skin and finely chop the flesh.

Preheat the oven to moderate 180°C (350°F/Gas 4). Grease 24 non-stick mini muffin holes. Sift the flour and baking powder, add the capsicum and Parmesan, and season. Make a well. Fold in the combined milk, eggs and oil with a metal spoon. Do not overmix — it should be lumpy.

Fill each muffin hole with the mixture. Bake for 15–20 minutes, or until a skewer comes out clean. Cool slightly, then lift out onto a wire rack.

Meanwhile, to make the tapenade, blend the olives, garlic, anchovies and capers in a food processor until finely chopped, then, while the motor is running, add the oil and lemon juice to form a paste. Season with pepper.

Heat the extra oil in a saucepan and fry the basil leaves until they are crisp. Remove and drain on paper towels.

While still warm, cut the tops off the muffins. Spread 1/2 teaspoon of mascarpone on each muffin, then add 1/2 teaspoon of tapenade. Top with a basil leaf before replacing the 'lids'.

Makes 24

Crumbed prawns with ponzu dipping sauce

18 raw large prawns
2 tablespoons cornflour
3 eggs
3 cups (240 g) fresh breadcrumbs
oil, for pan-frying
1/3 cup (80 ml) ponzu sauce or 1/4 cup
  (60 ml) soy sauce combined with
  1 tablespoon lemon juice

Peel and devein the prawns, leaving the tails intact. Cut down the back of each prawn to form a butterfly. Place each prawn between two layers of plastic wrap and gently beat to form a cutlet.

Put the cornflour, eggs and breadcrumbs in separate bowls. Lightly beat the eggs. Dip each prawn first into the cornflour then into the egg and finally into the breadcrumbs, ensuring that each cutlet is well covered in crumbs.

Heat the oil in a frying pan over medium heat until hot. Cook six prawn cutlets at a time for about 1 minute each side, or until the crumbs are golden—be careful they don't burn. Serve immediately with ponzu sauce.

Makes 18

Note: Ponzu is a Japanese dipping sauce usually used for sashimi.

Falafel

2 cups (440 g) dried chickpeas
1 onion, finely chopped
2 cloves garlic, crushed
2 tablespoons chopped fresh parsley
1 tablespoon chopped fresh coriander
2 teaspoons ground cumin
1/2 teaspoon baking powder
oil, for deep-frying

Soak the chickpeas in 3 cups (750 ml/24 fl oz) of water for 4 hours or overnight. Drain and place in a food processor, and process for 30 seconds, or until finely ground.

Add the onion, garlic, parsley, coriander, cumin, baking powder, 1 tablespoon of water, salt and pepper and process for 10 seconds, or until the mixture forms a rough paste. Cover and leave for 30 minutes.

Using your hands, shape heaped tablespoons of the falafel mixture into balls and squeeze out any excess liquid. Fill a deep heavy-based pan one-third full of oil to 180°C (350°F) and heat until a cube of bread browns in 15 seconds. Gently lower the falafel balls into the oil. Cook in batches of five at a time, for 3–4 minutes each batch. When the balls are browned, remove with a large slotted spoon. Drain well. Serve with Lebanese bread, tabbouleh and hummus.

Makes 30

Spiced carrot soup sip

1/3 cup (80 ml) olive oil
2 teaspoons honey
3 teaspoons ground cumin
3 teaspoons coriander seeds, lightly
  crushed
2 cinnamon sticks, broken in half
1.5 kg carrots, cut into even chunks
  (about 3 cm)
3 cups (750 ml) chicken stock
100 ml cream
3/4 cup (185 g) sour cream
3 tablespoons fresh coriander leaves

Preheat the oven to moderately hot 200°C (400°F/Gas 6). Combine the oil, honey, cumin, coriander seeds, cinnamon sticks, 1 teaspoon salt and plenty of cracked black pepper in a roasting tin. Add the chunks of carrot and mix well to ensure that all the carrot is coated in the spice mixture.

Roast for 1 hour, or until the carrot is tender, shaking the pan occasionally during cooking. Remove from the oven, discard the cinnamon sticks with tongs and allow the carrot to cool slightly.

Transfer half the carrot chunks, 1 1/2 cups (375 ml) of the stock and 1 cup (250 ml) water to a food processor or blender and blend until smooth. Strain through a fine sieve into a clean saucepan. Repeat with the remaining carrots, stock and another 1 cup (250 ml) water. Bring the soup to a simmer and cook for 10 minutes. Add the cream and season to taste. Pour into shot glasses or espresso cups. Garnish each cup with 1/4 teaspoon sour cream and a coriander leaf.

Serves 36 (Makes 1.25 litres)

Think ahead: The soup can be refrigerated for 2 days or frozen before the cream is added for up to 8 weeks.

Pork and noodle balls with sweet chilli sauce

Dipping sauce
⅓ cup (80 ml) sweet chilli sauce
2 teaspoons mirin
2 teaspoons finely chopped fresh
  ginger
½ cup (125 ml) Japanese soy sauce

250 g Hokkien noodles
300 g pork mince
6 spring onions, finely chopped
2 cloves garlic, crushed
⅓ cup (20 g) finely chopped fresh
  coriander leaves
1 tablespoon fish sauce
2 tablespoons oyster sauce
1½ tablespoons lime juice
peanut oil, for deep-frying

To make the dipping sauce, combine the sweet chilli sauce, mirin, ginger and Japanese soy sauce in a bowl.

Place the noodles in a bowl and cover with boiling water. Soak for 1 minute, or until tender. Drain very well and pat dry with paper towels. Cut the noodles into 5 cm lengths, then transfer to a large bowl. Add the pork mince, spring onion, garlic, coriander leaves, fish sauce, oyster sauce and lime juice and combine the mixture well using your hands, making sure the pork is evenly distributed throughout the noodles.

Roll a tablespoon of mixture at a time into a ball to make 30 in total, pressing each ball firmly to ensure they stick together during cooking.

Fill a wok or large saucepan one-third full of oil and heat to warm 170°C (325°F), or until a cube of bread browns in 20 seconds. Deep-fry the pork balls in batches for 2–3 minutes, or until golden and cooked through. Drain on paper towels. Serve hot with the dipping sauce.

Makes 30

Storage: The dipping sauce is best made up to a week in advance to allow the flavours to infuse.

Stuffed black olives

36 pitted jumbo black or large
   Kalamata olives (see Note)
100 g goat's cheese
1 teaspoon capers, drained and finely
   chopped
1 clove garlic, crushed
1 tablespoon chopped fresh flat-leaf
   parsley
1 1/2 tablespoons plain flour
2 eggs, lightly beaten
1 cup (100 g) dry breadcrumbs
1 tablespoon finely chopped fresh
   flat-leaf parsley, extra
oil, for deep-frying

Carefully cut the olives along the open cavity so they are opened out, but still in one piece.

Mash the goat's cheese, capers, garlic and parsley together in a small bowl, then season. Push an even amount of the mixture into the cavity of the olives, then press them closed.

Put the flour in one small bowl, the egg in another and combine the breadcrumbs and extra parsley in a third. Dip each olive first into the flour, then into the egg and, finally, into the breadcrumbs. Put the crumbed olives on a plate and refrigerate for at least 2 hours.

Fill a deep heavy-based saucepan or deep-fryer one-third full of oil and heat to 180°C (350°F), or until a cube of bread dropped into the oil browns in 15 seconds. Cook the olives in batches for 1–2 minutes, or until golden brown all over; you may need to turn them with tongs or a long-handled metal spoon. Drain on crumpled paper towels and season. Serve warm or at room temperature with lemon wedges.

Makes 36

Note: If you can't find large pitted olives, buy stuffed ones and remove the filling.

Roast beef on croûtes

300 g piece beef eye fillet
1/3 cup (80 ml) olive oil
2 cloves garlic, crushed
2 sprigs fresh thyme, plus extra
  to garnish
10 slices white bread
1 large clove garlic, peeled, extra

Horseradish cream
1/3 cup (80 ml) thick cream
1 tablespoon horseradish
1 teaspoon lemon juice

Place the beef in a non-metallic bowl, add the combined oil, garlic and thyme and toss to coat. Cover and chill for 3 hours. Preheat the oven to moderately hot 200°C (400°F/Gas 6).

Cut three rounds from each slice of bread using a 5 cm fluted cutter. Place on a baking tray and bake for 5 minutes each side, then rub the whole garlic clove over each side of the rounds.

To make the horseradish cream, whisk the cream lightly until thickened. Fold in the horseradish and lemon juice, then season with cracked black pepper. Refrigerate until ready to use.

Heat a roasting tin in the oven for 5 minutes. Season the beef on all sides, then place in the hot roasting tin and turn it so that the surface of the meat is sealed. Drizzle with 2 tablespoons of the reserved marinade, then roast for 10 minutes for rare, or until the meat is cooked to your liking. Remove from the oven, cover with foil and rest for 15 minutes before slicing thinly.

Arrange a slice of beef on each croûte, top with 1/2 teaspoon of the horseradish cream and a small sprig of fresh thyme. Serve immediately.

Makes 30

Creamed egg with roe tartlets

Basic pastry cases
2 cups (250 g) plain flour
125 g chilled butter, chopped
1 egg

4 eggs and 4 egg yolks
75 g unsalted butter
4 tablespoons roe

Preheat the oven to moderately hot 200°C (400°F/Gas 6). Lightly grease 30 mini muffin holes. Sift the flour into a large bowl and rub the butter in with your fingertips until the mixture resembles fine breadcrumbs. Make a well in the centre, add the egg and mix with a flat-bladed knife, using a cutting action until it comes together in beads. If the dough seems too dry, add a little cold water. Press the dough into a ball on a lightly floured surface, then wrap it in plastic wrap and refrigerate for 30 minutes.

Roll out the dough between two sheets of baking paper to 2 mm thick and cut out 30 rounds with a 6 cm cutter. Press a round into each muffin hole. Prick the bases with a fork and bake for 6–8 minutes, or until dry and golden. If they puff up, use a clean tea towel to press out the air. Cool.

Lightly beat the eggs and egg yolks together. Melt the butter over very low heat, then add the eggs and whisk slowly and constantly for 5–6 minutes, or until the mixture is thick and creamy but the eggs are not scrambled. Remove from the heat straight away and season to taste. Fill each pastry case with 1 teaspoon of the creamed egg mixture, then top with 1/2 teaspoon of roe before serving.

Makes 30

Won ton stacks with tuna and ginger

1 1/2 tablespoons sesame seeds
12 fresh won ton wrappers
1/2 cup (125 ml) peanut or vegetable
  oil
150 g piece fresh tuna fillet (see Note)
1/4 cup (60 g) Japanese mayonnaise
50 g pickled ginger
50 g snow pea (mangetout) sprouts
2 teaspoons mirin
2 teaspoons soy sauce
1/4 teaspoon sugar

Lightly toast the sesame seeds in a small dry frying pan over low heat for 2–3 minutes, or until golden.

Cut the won ton wrappers into quarters to give 48 squares in total. Heat the oil in a small saucepan over medium heat and cook the wrappers in batches for 1–2 minutes, or until they are golden and crisp. Drain on crumpled paper towels.

Thinly slice the tuna into 24 slices. Spoon approximately 1/4 teaspoon of the mayonnaise onto 24 of the won ton squares. Place a slice of tuna on the mayonnaise and top with a little of the pickled ginger, snow pea sprouts and sesame seeds.

Mix the mirin, soy sauce and sugar together in a small bowl and drizzle a little over each stack. Season with pepper. Top with the remaining 24 won ton squares. Serve straight away, or the stacks will become soggy.

Makes 24

Note: For this recipe, you need good-quality tuna. Sashimi tuna is the best quality, but if you can't get that, get tuna with as little sinew as possible. Think ahead: The won ton wrappers can be fried the day before serving. Store them in an airtight container with paper towels between each layer.

Salmon cakes with herb mayonnaise

500 g salmon fillet, skin and bones
  removed, cut into 5 mm cubes
3 tablespoons dry breadcrumbs
1 tablespoon lightly beaten egg
1/2 teaspoon finely grated lime zest
3 1/2 teaspoons lime juice
3 teaspoons fresh dill, chopped
1/2 cup (125 g) whole-egg mayonnaise
1 clove garlic, crushed
2 tablespoons light olive oil

Place the salmon, breadcrumbs, egg, lime zest, 3 teaspoons lime juice and 2 teaspoons dill in a bowl. Stir until the mixture comes together and the ingredients are evenly distributed. Season well with salt and freshly ground black pepper.

With wet hands, using 2 heaped teaspoons of mixture at a time, shape into 36 small round cakes. Place on a baking tray lined with baking paper. Refrigerate until ready to use.

For the herb mayonnaise, mix the remaining lime juice and dill with the mayonnaise and garlic in a bowl.

Heat the olive oil in a large non-stick frying pan. Cook the salmon cakes in batches over medium heat for 2 minutes each side, or until golden and cooked through. Do not overcook. Drain on paper towels. Top each with a little of the herb mayonnaise and season well. Serve immediately, garnished with lime strips if desired.

Makes 36

Variation: You can also top these with 1/2 cup (125 g) crème fraîche and 1 1/2 tablespoons salmon roe.

Thai chicken sausage rolls

200 g chicken breast fillet, roughly
  chopped
150 g mild pancetta, chopped
1 clove garlic, crushed
3 spring onions, chopped
2 tablespoons chopped fresh
  coriander
2 bird's eye chillies, seeded and
  finely chopped
1 teaspoon fish sauce
1 egg
1 teaspoon grated fresh ginger
375 g block frozen puff pastry
1 egg yolk
2 tablespoons sesame seeds
sweet chilli sauce, to serve
fresh coriander, to serve

Preheat the oven to moderate 180°C
(350°F/Gas 4). Put the chicken,
pancetta, garlic, spring onion,
coriander, chilli, fish sauce, whole
egg and ginger in a food processor
and process until just combined.

Roll out the pastry to an oblong
30 x 40 cm. Cut in half lengthways.
Take half the filling and, using floured
hands, roll it into a long sausage
shape and place along the long
edge of one piece of pastry. Brush
the edges with a little water and fold
over, pressing down to seal. Place the
sealed edge underneath. Repeat with
the remaining pastry and filling.

Using a sharp knife, cut the sausage
rolls into 3 cm lengths on the diagonal;
discard the end pieces. Brush the
tops with egg yolk, then sprinkle with
sesame seeds. Bake for 15 minutes,
or until golden. Serve with sweet chilli
sauce and garnished with coriander.

Makes 24

Think ahead: You can make the
sausage rolls a day before the party.
Reheat in a moderate (180°C/350°F/
Gas 4) oven for 10–12 minutes, or
until warmed through.

Stuffed chillies

1 teaspoon cumin seeds
12 mild small jalapeño or similar mild
  oblong-shaped fat chillies,
  approximately 4 cm x 3 cm
1 tablespoon olive oil
2 cloves garlic, finely chopped
½ small red onion, finely chopped
½ cup (125 g) cream cheese,
  softened
¼ cup (30 g) coarsely grated Cheddar
2 tablespoons finely chopped drained
  sun-dried tomatoes
1 tablespoon chopped fresh coriander
1 teaspoon finely chopped lime zest
pinch of smoked paprika
½ cup (50 g) coarse dry breadcrumbs
2 teaspoons lime juice
coriander leaves, to garnish

Preheat the oven to moderately hot 200°C (400°F/Gas 6). Line a baking tray with baking paper. Toast the cumin seeds in a dry frying pan for 1–2 minutes, or until fragrant. Cool slightly, then grind the seeds.

Cut the chillies lengthways through the middle. Wearing gloves, remove the seeds and membranes. Bring a saucepan of water to the boil, add the chillies and cook for 1 minute, or until the water comes back to the boil. Drain, rinse under cold water, then return to a saucepan of fresh boiling water for another minute before draining, rinsing, then draining again.

Heat the oil in a non-stick frying pan and cook the garlic and onion over medium–low heat for 4–5 minutes, or until the onion softens. Mash the cream cheese in a bowl, add the Cheddar, sun-dried tomato, coriander, lime zest, paprika, cumin and half the breadcrumbs, and mix well. Stir in the onion and season. Fill each chilli with one heaped teaspoon of the mixture, then lay on the baking tray and scatter with the remaining breadcrumbs.

Bake for 20 minutes. Squeeze some lime juice over the top and garnish with coriander leaves.

Makes 24

212

Vegetable dumplings

8 dried Chinese mushrooms
1 tablespoon oil
2 teaspoons finely chopped fresh
    ginger
2 garlic cloves, crushed
100 g Chinese chives, chopped
100 g water spinach, cut into 1 cm
    lengths
1/4 cup (60 ml) chicken stock
2 tablespoons oyster sauce
1 tablespoon cornflour
1 teaspoon soy sauce
1 teaspoon rice wine
1/4 cup (45 g) water chestnuts,
    chopped
chilli sauce, to serve

Wrappers
200 g wheat starch
1 teaspoon cornflour
oil, for kneading

Soak the mushrooms in hot water for 15 minutes. Finely chop the caps. Heat the oil in a frying pan over high heat, add the ginger, garlic and a pinch of salt and white pepper. Cook for 30 seconds. Add the chives and spinach and cook for 1 minute.

Combine the stock, oyster sauce, cornflour, soy sauce and rice wine, and add to the spinach mixture with the water chestnuts and mushrooms. Cook for 1 minute, or until thickened, then cool completely.

To make the wrappers, combine the wheat starch and cornflour. Make a well and add 3/4 cup (185 ml) boiling water, a little at a time, bringing the mixture together with your hands. Knead with lightly oiled hands until the dough forms a shiny ball.

Keep the dough covered while you work. Roll out walnut-sized pieces of dough into very thin 10 cm diameter circles. Place 1 tablespoon of filling in the centre. Pinch the edges together to form a tight ball.

Put the dumplings in a bamboo steamer lined with baking paper, leaving a gap between each one. Cover and steam for 7–8 minutes. Serve with chilli sauce.

Makes 24

Won ton wrapped prawns

24 raw medium prawns
1 teaspoon cornflour
24 won ton wrappers
oil, for deep-frying
1/2 cup (125 ml) sweet chilli sauce
1 tablespoon lime juice

Peel the prawns, leaving the tails intact. Pull out the dark vein from each back, starting at the head end.

Mix the cornflour with 1 teaspoon water in a small bowl. Fold each won ton wrapper in half to form a triangle. Cover them with a tea towel while you are working, to prevent them drying out. Wrap each prawn in a wrapper, leaving the tail exposed. Seal at the end by brushing on a little of the cornflour mixture, then pressing gently. Spread the wrapped prawns on a baking tray, cover with plastic wrap and refrigerate for 20 minutes.

Fill a deep heavy-based saucepan one-third full of oil and heat to 180°C (350°F), or until a cube of bread dropped into the oil browns in 15 seconds. Cook the prawns in batches for 1 1/2 minutes each batch, or until crisp, golden and cooked through. The cooking time may vary depending on the size of the prawns. Determine the correct time by cooking one prawn and testing it before continuing. Remove the prawns from the oil and drain on crumpled paper towels.

Stir the sweet chilli sauce and lime juice together in a small bowl. Serve with the prawns.

Makes 24

Steamed pork buns

1 cup (250 ml) milk
½ cup (125 g) caster sugar
3 cups (450 g) char sui pork bun flour
  (see Note)
1 tablespoon oil

Filling
2 teaspoons oil
1 clove garlic, crushed
2 spring onions, finely chopped
3 teaspoons cornflour
2 teaspoons hoisin sauce
1½ teaspoons soy sauce
½ teaspoon caster sugar
150 g Chinese barbecued pork,
  finely chopped

Combine the milk and sugar, and stir over low heat until dissolved. Sift all but two tablespoons of flour into a bowl and make a well. Gradually add the milk, stirring until it just comes together. Dust a work surface with the reserved flour and knead the dough for 10 minutes, or until elastic. Knead the oil into the dough a little at a time, kneading for 10 minutes. Cover with plastic wrap and chill for 30 minutes.

For the filling, heat the oil in a pan, add the garlic and spring onion and stir over medium heat until just soft. Blend the cornflour with ⅓ cup (80 ml) water, the sauces and sugar, and add to the pan. Stir over medium heat until the mixture boils and thickens. Remove from the heat and stir in the pork. Allow to cool.

Divide the dough into 24 portions and flatten, so the edges are thinner than the centre. Place teaspoons of filling on each and pull up the edges around the filling, pinching firmly to seal. Place each bun on a square of greaseproof paper and place 3 cm apart in a bamboo steamer. Steam in batches for 15 minutes, or until the buns have risen and are cooked through.

Makes about 24

Note: Buy char sui pork bun flour at Asian food stores.

Salt and pepper squid

1 kg squid tubes, halved lengthways
  (see Note)
1 cup (250 ml) lemon juice
1 cup (125 g) cornflour
1½ tablespoons salt
1 tablespoon ground white pepper
2 teaspoons caster sugar
4 egg whites, lightly beaten
oil, for deep-frying
lemon wedges, for serving

Open out the squid tubes, then wash and pat dry. Lay on a chopping board with the inside facing upwards. Score a fine diamond pattern on the inside, being careful not to cut all the way through. Cut the squid into pieces measuring 5 cm x 2 cm. Place in a flat non-metallic dish and pour on the lemon juice. Cover and refrigerate for 15 minutes. Drain well and pat dry.

Combine the cornflour, salt, white pepper and sugar in a bowl. Dip the squid into the egg white and lightly coat with the cornflour mixture, shaking off any excess.

Fill a deep heavy-based saucepan or deep-fryer one-third full of oil and heat to 180°C (350°F), or until a cube of bread dropped into the oil turns golden brown in 15 seconds. Deep-fry the squid, in batches, for 1 minute each batch, or until the squid turns lightly golden and curls up. Drain on crumpled paper towels. Serve with lemon wedges.

Serves 12

Note: If you are cleaning the squid yourself, reserve the tentacles, cut them into groups of two or three depending on the size; marinate and cook them with the tubes.

Mini corn muffins with Cajun fish

Muffins

3/4 cup (90 g) self-raising flour
2 tablespoons cornflour
1/2 teaspoon baking powder
1/2 cup (75 g) fine cornmeal
2 tablespoons sugar
2/3 cup (170 ml) milk
1 egg
30 g butter, melted
20 g butter, extra

1 teaspoon onion powder
1 teaspoon dried thyme
3/4 teaspoon sea salt flakes
1/2 teaspoon garlic powder
1/4 teaspoon cayenne pepper
1/4 teaspoon dried oregano
400 g bream or white fish fillets,
    skinned
30 g butter
1/2 cup (125 g) sour cream
coriander leaves, to garnish

Preheat the oven to moderate 180°C (350°F/Gas 4). Lightly grease 24 non-stick mini muffin holes. Sift the flour, cornflour and baking powder into a bowl. Stir in the cornmeal and sugar. Make a well in the centre. Pour the combined milk and egg into the well, then the melted butter. Fold gently with a metal spoon until just combined and still a little lumpy.

Fill each muffin hole about three-quarters full. Bake for 15–20 minutes, or until golden. Before removing from the oven, melt the extra butter. Brush the muffins with the butter, then remove from the tin and cool.

Combine the spices and herbs and 1/4 teaspoon cracked black pepper. Slice the fish into 1.5 cm slices and coat well in the spice mixture.

Melt the butter in a stainless steel frying pan (not non-stick) over medium heat and add the fish when the butter is foaming. Cook the fish, turning once, for 1–2 minutes, or until it starts to blacken, and is cooked.

To serve, cut a small wedge in the top of the muffins, then put in 1/2 teaspoon of sour cream, then add a piece of fish and a coriander leaf. Serve while the fish is hot.

Makes 24

Arancini

2 cups (440 g) risotto rice
1 egg, lightly beaten
1 egg yolk
1/2 cup (50 g) grated Parmesan
plain flour
2 eggs, lightly beaten
dry breadcrumbs, to coat
oil, for deep-frying

Meat sauce
1 dried porcini mushroom
1 tablespoon olive oil
1 onion, chopped
125 g minced beef or veal
2 slices prosciutto, finely chopped
2 tablespoons tomato paste (purée)
1/3 cup (80 ml) white wine
1/2 teaspoon dried thyme leaves
3 tablespoons finely chopped fresh
  parsley

Cook the rice in boiling water for
20 minutes, or until just soft. Drain,
without rinsing, and cool. Put in
a large bowl and add the egg, egg
yolk and Parmesan. Stir until the rice
sticks together. Cover and set aside.

To make the meat sauce, soak the
mushroom in hot water for 10 minutes
to soften, then squeeze dry and chop
finely. Heat the oil in a frying pan. Add
the mushroom and onion and cook
for 3 minutes, or until soft. Add the
mince and cook, stirring, until
browned. Add the prosciutto, tomato
paste, wine, thyme and pepper to
taste. Cook, stirring, for 5 minutes,
or until all the liquid is absorbed. Stir
in the parsley and set aside to cool.

With wet hands, form the rice mixture
into 10 balls. Wet your hands again
and gently pull the balls apart. Place
3 teaspoons of the meat sauce in the
centre of each. Reshape to enclose
the filling. Roll in the flour, beaten egg
and breadcrumbs and chill for 1 hour.

Fill a deep heavy-based pan one-third
full of oil and heat to 180°C (350°F),
or until a cube of bread browns in
15 seconds. Deep-fry the croquettes,
two at a time, for 3–4 minutes, or until
golden brown. Drain on paper towels
and keep warm while cooking the rest.

Makes 10

Lentil patties with cumin skordalia

1 cup (185 g) brown lentils
1 teaspoon cumin seeds
1/2 cup (90 g) burghul (bulgur wheat)
1 tablespoon olive oil
3 cloves garlic, crushed
4 spring onions, thinly sliced
1 teaspoon ground coriander
3 tablespoons chopped fresh parsley
3 tablespoons chopped fresh mint
2 eggs, lightly beaten
oil, for deep-frying

Skordalia
500 g floury potatoes, cut into
  2 cm cubes
3 cloves garlic, crushed
1/2 teaspoon ground cumin
pinch of ground white pepper
3/4 cup (185 ml) olive oil
2 tablespoons white vinegar

Place the lentils in a saucepan, add 2 1/2 cups (625 ml) water and bring to the boil. Reduce the heat to low and cook, covered, for 30 minutes, or until soft. Meanwhile, toast the cumin in a dry frying pan over low heat for 1–2 minutes, or until fragrant. Grind.

Remove the lentils from the heat and stir in the burghul. Set aside to cool.

Heat the oil in a frying pan and cook the garlic and spring onion for 1 minute. Add the coriander and cumin and cook for 30 seconds. Add to the lentil mixture with the parsley, mint and egg. Mix well. Chill for 30 minutes.

To make the skordalia, cook the potato in a saucepan of boiling water for 10 minutes, or until very soft. Drain and mash until smooth. Add the garlic, cumin, white pepper and 1 teaspoon salt. Gradually add the oil, mixing with a wooden spoon. Add the vinegar.

Roll tablespoons of the lentil mixture into balls, then flatten slightly. Fill a deep heavy-based saucepan or deep-fryer one-third full of oil and heat to 180°C (350°F), or until a cube of bread browns in 15 seconds. Cook the patties in batches for 1–2 minutes, or until crisp and browned. Drain on paper towels. Serve with the skordalia.

Makes 32

Scallops on potato crisps with pea purée

1 tablespoon butter
3 French shallots, finely chopped
1 clove garlic, finely chopped
2 slices mild pancetta, finely chopped
1 cup (155 g) frozen peas
¼ cup (60 ml) chicken stock or water
oil, for deep-frying, plus 1 tablespoon
4–5 floury potatoes (e.g. russet, King Edward), peeled and very thinly sliced to get 48 slices
24 scallops, cut in half horizontally through the centre
fresh mint, to garnish

Melt the butter in a small saucepan and fry the shallots, garlic and pancetta over low heat for 3 minutes, or until soft but not coloured. Add the peas and stock, and cook over high heat for 3 minutes, or until all the liquid has evaporated. Cool a little, transfer to a food processor and purée until smooth. Season.

Fill a deep heavy-based saucepan or deep-fryer one-third full of oil and heat to 190°C (375°F), or until a cube of bread dropped into the oil browns in 10 seconds. Cook the potato slices in batches until crisp and golden. Drain on crumpled paper towels and sprinkle with salt.

Toss the scallops with 1 tablespoon oil. Season lightly. Heat a chargrill pan to hot, then sear the scallops in batches for 5 seconds each side, or until lightly browned on the outside but opaque in the middle.

Reheat the pea purée. Dollop 1 teaspoon of purée on each potato crisp, then top with a scallop. Season with pepper and garnish with mint.

Makes 48

Think ahead: The purée can be made 2 days early and refrigerated. The crisps can be cooked 2 hours early; store in an airtight container.

Bitterballen

1¾ cups (440 ml) beef stock
1 small carrot, very finely diced
½ celery stick, very finely diced
1 small onion, very finely diced
1 bay leaf
50 g butter
50 g plain flour
300 g beef or veal mince
3 cloves garlic, crushed
1 tablespoon finely chopped fresh
  parsley
1 tablespoon Worcestershire sauce
2 teaspoons ground nutmeg
1 teaspoon lemon zest, finely minced
dry breadcrumbs, to coat
3 eggs, beaten
oil, for deep-frying
English mustard, to serve

Place the stock, carrot, celery, onion and bay leaf in a saucepan and bring to the boil over high heat. Simmer for 10 minutes. Strain, reserving all the solids except the bay leaf.

Melt the butter over medium heat in a large saucepan. Add the flour, mix well and cook for 1 minute. Gradually add the warm stock, stirring constantly until you have a thick, smooth sauce. Reduce the heat to low.

Add the mince, garlic, parsley, Worcestershire sauce, nutmeg, lemon zest, reserved vegetables, 1 teaspoon salt and ½ teaspoon cracked black pepper. Cook over low heat for 15 minutes, stirring regularly. Cool slightly, then transfer to a clean dish. Cover and chill overnight or until the mixture is well chilled and firm.

Roll heaped teaspoons of the mixture into balls. Roll in breadcrumbs, then in the egg, then again in breadcrumbs. Chill the finished balls as you work. Refrigerate the balls for at least 1 hour.

Fill a large heavy-based saucepan one-third full of oil and heat to 190°C (375°F), or until a cube of bread browns in 10 seconds. Deep-fry the balls for 4 minutes, or until golden. Serve immediately with mustard.

Makes about 60

Honey mustard chicken drumettes

1/3 cup (80 ml) oil
1/4 cup (90 g) honey
1/4 cup (60 ml) soy sauce
1/4 cup (60 g) Dijon mustard
1/4 cup (60 ml) lemon juice
4 cloves garlic, crushed
24 chicken drumettes (see Note)

To make the marinade, place the oil, honey, soy sauce, mustard, lemon juice and garlic in a large non-metallic dish and mix together thoroughly.

Trim the chicken of excess fat, then place in the dish with the marinade and toss until well coated. Cover and refrigerate for at least 2 hours, or preferably overnight, turning 2–3 times.

Preheat the oven to moderately hot 200°C (400°F/Gas 6). Place the drumettes on a wire rack over a foil-lined baking tray. Bake, turning and brushing with the marinade 3–4 times, for 45 minutes, or until golden brown and cooked. Serve immediately with serviettes for sticky fingers.

Makes 24

Note: Drumettes are the chicken wing with the wing tip removed.
Think ahead: Cook a day ahead and reheat in a warm 160°C (315°F/Gas 2–3) oven for 10–12 minutes.
Variation: For a teriyaki marinade, combine 1/2 cup (125 ml) teriyaki sauce, 1/4 cup (60 ml) pineapple juice, 2 tablespoons honey, 1 tablespoon grated fresh ginger, 2 cloves crushed garlic and 1 teaspoon sesame oil.

Spinach and feta triangles

1 kg English spinach
1/4 cup (60 ml) olive oil
1 onion, chopped
10 spring onions, sliced
1/3 cup (20 g) chopped fresh parsley
1 tablespoon chopped fresh dill
large pinch of ground nutmeg
1/3 cup (35 g) grated Parmesan
150 g crumbled feta cheese
90 g ricotta cheese
4 eggs, lightly beaten
40 g butter, melted
1 tablespoon olive oil, extra
12 sheets filo pastry

Trim any stems from the spinach. Wash the leaves, roughly chop and place in a large pan with a little water clinging to the leaves. Cover and cook over low heat for 5 minutes, or until the leaves have wilted. Drain well and allow to cool slightly before squeezing to remove the excess water.

Heat the oil in a heavy-based frying pan. Add the onion and cook over low heat for 10 minutes, or until tender and golden. Add the spring onion and cook for a further 3 minutes. Remove from the heat. Stir in the spinach, parsley, dill, nutmeg, Parmesan, feta, ricotta and egg. Season well.

Preheat the oven to moderate 180°C (350°F/Gas 4). Grease two baking trays. Combine the butter with the extra oil. Work with three sheets of pastry at a time, covering the rest with a damp tea towel. Brush each sheet with butter mixture and lay them on top of each other. Halve lengthways.

Place 4 tablespoons of filling on an angle at the end of each strip. Fold the pastry to enclose the filling and form a triangle. Continue folding the triangle over until you reach the end. Brush with the remaining butter mixture and bake for 20 minutes, or until golden brown.

Makes 8

Macadamia-crusted chicken strips

12 chicken tenderloins (700 g), larger
  ones cut in half
seasoned plain flour, to dust
2 eggs, lightly beaten
250 g macadamia nuts, finely
  chopped
2 cups (160 g) fresh breadcrumbs
oil, to deep-fry

Cut the chicken into strips. First, dust the chicken strips with the flour, then dip them in the egg and, finally, coat them in the combined nuts and breadcrumbs. Refrigerate for at least 30 minutes to firm up.

Fill a large heavy-based saucepan or deep-fryer one-third full of oil and heat to 180°C (350°F), or until a cube of bread dropped in the oil browns in 15 seconds. Cook the chicken in batches for 2–3 minutes, or until golden brown all over, taking care not to burn the nuts. Drain on crumpled paper towels. Serve warm.

Makes 24

Variations: The chicken strips are very tasty served with sweet chilli sauce or a mango salsa. Try making your own salsa by combining one small, finely diced mango, 2 tablespoons finely diced red onion, 2 tablespoons roughly chopped, fresh coriander leaves, one fresh green chilli, seeded and finely chopped, and 1 tablespoon of lime juice. Season to taste. Try a different coating using almonds or peanuts.

Spicy corn puffs

2 corn cobs
3 tablespoons chopped fresh
  coriander leaves
6 spring onions, finely chopped
1 small red chilli, seeded and finely
  chopped
1 large egg
2 teaspoons ground cumin
1/2 teaspoon ground coriander
1 cup (125 g) plain flour
oil, for deep-frying
sweet chilli sauce, to serve

Cut down the side of the corn with a sharp knife to release the kernels. Roughly chop the kernels, then place them in a large bowl. Holding the cobs over the bowl, scrape down the sides of the cobs with a knife to release any corn juice from the cob into the bowl.

Add the fresh coriander, spring onion, chilli, egg, cumin, ground coriander, 1 teaspoon salt and some cracked black pepper to the bowl and stir well. Add the flour and mix well. The texture of the batter will vary depending on the juiciness of the corn. If the mixture is too dry, add 1 tablespoon water, but no more than that as the batter should be quite dry. Stand for 10 minutes.

Fill a large heavy-based saucepan or deep-fryer one-third full of oil and heat to 180°C (350°F), or until a cube of bread dropped in the oil browns in 15 seconds. Drop slightly heaped teaspoons of the corn batter into the oil and cook for about 1 1/2 minutes, or until puffed and golden. Drain on crumpled paper towels and serve immediately with a bowl of the sweet chilli sauce to dip the puffs into.

Makes about 36

Note: The corn puffs should be prepared just before serving.

Sesame beef skewers

½ cup (125 ml) soy sauce
⅓ cup (80 ml) Chinese rice wine
2 cloves garlic, crushed
1 teaspoon finely grated fresh ginger
1 teaspoon sesame oil
225 g beef fillet, cut into
  2 cm cubes
8 spring onions
2 tablespoons toasted sesame seeds

Combine the soy sauce, wine, garlic, ginger and oil, and pour over the beef. Marinate for 20 minutes. Drain, reserving the marinade.

Cut six of the spring onions into 24 x 3 cm pieces and thread a piece plus two meat cubes onto 24 skewers. Cook on a hot barbecue hotplate or chargrill pan for 5 minutes, or until cooked. Remove, sprinkle with sesame seeds and keep warm.

Put the reserved marinade in a saucepan and bring to the boil for 1 minute, then add 2 thinly sliced spring onions. Pour into a bowl and serve with the skewers.

Makes 24

Basil mussels

1 kg black mussels
10 g butter
2 red Asian shallots, chopped
½ cup (125 ml) dry white wine

Basil butter
50 g butter
10 g fresh basil leaves
1 clove garlic, chopped
2 tablespoons dry breadcrumbs

Scrub the mussels with a stiff brush and pull out the hairy beards. Discard any broken mussels or open ones that don't close when tapped on the bench. Rinse well.

Melt the butter in a large saucepan over medium heat. Add the shallots and cook for 2 minutes, or until soft. Add the wine and mussels, increase the heat and cook for 4–5 minutes, stirring occasionally, until the mussels have opened. Remove the open mussels and discard unopened ones.

For the basil butter, process all the ingredients together in a food processor or blender until smooth. Season with ground black pepper.

Separate the mussel shells, leaving the meat on one half. Discard the empty shells. Place a teaspoon of basil butter on each mussel. Arrange on a foil-lined grill tray and cook under a hot grill for 1 minute, or until the butter is melted. Season with salt and ground black pepper, to taste.

Serves 6

Variation: Use scallops on the half shell—remove hard muscle, continue from step 3 and grill for 2 minutes.

Turkish bread with herbed zucchini

½ large loaf Turkish bread
1 tablespoon sesame seeds
½ cup (125 ml) vegetable oil

Herbed zucchini
1 tablespoon olive oil
2 cloves garlic, finely chopped
4 x 100 g small zucchini (courgette), roughly chopped
1 large carrot, thinly sliced
2 tablespoons chopped fresh flat-leaf parsley
2 tablespoons chopped fresh mint
2 teaspoons lemon juice
½ teaspoon ground cumin

Split the bread horizontally through the middle and open it out. Cut the bread into 3 cm squares; you should end up with 48 squares.

Toast the sesame seeds in a large dry non-stick frying pan over low heat for 2–3 minutes, or until golden. Remove from the pan. Heat the vegetable oil in the same pan and cook the bread in batches for 1–2 minutes each side, or until crisp and golden. Drain on paper towels.

Heat the olive oil in a saucepan over medium heat and cook the garlic for 1 minute. Add the zucchini and carrot and cook over medium heat for 2 minutes. Season with salt and pepper. Add 1 tablespoon water, cover and simmer over low heat for 15 minutes, or until the vegetables are soft. Spoon into a bowl and mash roughly with a potato masher. Add the parsley, mint, lemon juice and cumin. Season to taste.

Spoon 2 teaspoons of the zucchini mixture over each square of bread and scatter with sesame seeds. Serve warm or at room temperature.

Makes 48

Think ahead: The herbed zucchini can be prepared up to 2 days in advance. Reheat just before serving.

Caramelised red onion and feta tartlets

1½ tablespoons olive oil
2 large red onions, finely chopped
2 teaspoons chopped fresh thyme
3 sheets ready-rolled shortcrust
    pastry
70 g feta cheese, crumbled
2 eggs, lightly beaten
½ cup (125 ml) cream

Preheat the oven to moderate 180°C (350°F/Gas 4). Heat the oil in a frying pan (do not use a non-stick one or the onion won't caramelise). Add the onion and cook, stirring occasionally, over medium–low heat for 30 minutes, or until dark gold. Add the thyme, stir well and transfer to a bowl to cool.

Grease 24 shallow patty tin holes. Using an 8 cm cutter, cut out 24 pastry rounds and line the tins with the rounds.

Divide the onion among the patty cases, then spoon the feta over the onion. Combine the eggs with the cream, season and pour into the pastry cases. Bake for 10–15 minutes, or until puffed and golden. Leave in the tins for 5 minutes before transferring to a wire rack to cool.

Makes 24

Think ahead: These can be made a day in advance and reheated in a slow (150°C/300°F/Gas 2) oven for 10 minutes before serving.

Whitebait fritters with tartare sauce

1 cup (125 g) plain flour
1 large egg, lightly beaten
1 cup (250 ml) iced water
3 tablespoons chopped fresh parsley
3 teaspoons grated lemon zest
400 g whitebait
oil, for deep-frying

Tartare sauce
2 egg yolks
1 teaspoon Dijon mustard
1 cup (250 ml) olive oil
1 tablespoon lemon juice
2 tablespoons capers, drained and
  chopped
2 tablespoons chopped gherkins
1 tablespoon chopped fresh parsley
1 tablespoon chopped fresh tarragon

Sift the flour and a pinch of salt and pepper into a large bowl, make a well in the centre and add the egg. Whisk gently and gradually add the water, stirring constantly to a smooth batter. Stir in the parsley and lemon zest. Refrigerate, covered, for 1 hour.

To make the tartare sauce, place the egg yolks and mustard in a food processor and pulse for 10 seconds. With the motor running, slowly add the oil in a thin stream until the mixture is thick and creamy. Add the lemon juice and 2 teaspoons boiling water and pulse for another 10 seconds. Transfer to a bowl, add the capers, gherkins, parsley and tarragon and season generously. Cover and refrigerate until needed.

Pat the whitebait dry, then gently stir into the batter. Fill a large heavy-based saucepan one-third full of oil and heat to 190°C (375°F), or until a cube of bread dropped in the oil browns in 10 seconds. Put small tablespoons of batter into the oil. Cook the fritters in batches, gently tossing in the oil. Cook for 2 minutes, or until the fritters are golden brown. Drain on crumpled paper towels and keep warm. Repeat with the remaining mixture. Serve immediately with the tartare sauce.

Makes 50

Steamed prawn rice noodle rolls

Dipping sauce
2 tablespoons light soy sauce
3 tablespoons rice vinegar

3 dried shiitake mushrooms
350 g raw prawns, peeled and
  deveined
4 spring onions, chopped
60 g snow peas (mangetout),
  chopped
2 teaspoons finely chopped fresh
  ginger
2 cloves garlic, crushed
1/2 cup (15 g) chopped fresh coriander
  leaves
100 g water chestnuts, chopped
1 teaspoon sesame oil
1 tablespoon light soy sauce
1 egg white
1 teaspoon cornflour
300 g fresh rice noodle rolls

To make the dipping sauce, combine the soy sauce and rice vinegar.

Cover the mushrooms with hot water and soak for 15 minutes. Drain, discard the stalks, and finely chop the caps.

Mince the prawns in a food processor. Add the mushrooms, spring onion, snow peas, ginger, garlic, coriander, water chestnuts, sesame oil, soy sauce and a pinch of salt. Add the egg white and cornflour and pulse until smooth.

Line a large bamboo steamer with baking paper and place over a wok of simmering water (ensure the base doesn't touch the water). Gently unfold the rice sheet noodle and cut into six 15 cm squares. Spread 1/4 cup (60 ml) filling evenly over each square and roll firmly to form a log. Steam, covered, in a wok for 5 minutes. Cut each roll in half and serve with the sauce.

Makes 12

Rösti with smoked trout and salsa verde

1 small smoked trout
450 g floury potatoes (e.g. russet,
  King Edward or pontiac)
2 spring onions, thinly sliced
⅓ cup (80 ml) olive oil

Salsa verde
1½ cups (30 g) fresh flat-leaf parsley
1 cup (30 g) fresh basil
1 tablespoon capers, drained
1 tablespoon chopped gherkin or
  4 cornichons (baby gherkins)
2 anchovies, drained
1 clove garlic, chopped
2 teaspoons Dijon mustard
¼ cup (60 ml) olive oil
1 tablespoon lemon juice

Remove the skin from the trout, pull the flesh from the bones and flake into pieces.

To make the salsa verde, place the parsley, basil, capers, gherkin, anchovies, garlic and mustard in a food processor and blend until finely chopped. While the motor is running, blend in the oil and lemon juice until mixed together. Season with pepper.

To make the rösti, peel and coarsely grate the potatoes. Squeeze out as much liquid as possible. Mix the flesh in a bowl with the spring onion. Heat the oil in a large heavy-based frying pan over medium–high heat. To cook the rösti, take heaped teaspoons of the potato mixture, add to the pan in batches and press down with an egg flip to help the potato stay together. Cook for 2–3 minutes each side, or until crisp and golden. Drain on crumpled paper towels.

Top each rösti with a teaspoon of salsa verde then some flakes of trout. Serve warm or at room temperature.

Makes 32

Think ahead: The rösti can be made 8 hours beforehand and kept in an airtight container lined with paper towels. Reheat for 5 minutes in a moderate (180°C/350°F/Gas 4) oven.

Polenta wedges with bocconcini and tomato

1 tablespoon olive oil
1²/₃ cups (250 g) polenta
³/₄ cup (75 g) grated Parmesan
2¹/₂ tablespoons ready-made pesto
150 g bocconcini, thinly sliced
12 cherry tomatoes, cut into quarters
¹/₂ cup (15 g) fresh basil, larger
  leaves torn

Lightly grease a 20 cm x 30 cm baking tin with the olive oil. Bring 1 litre lightly salted water to the boil in a saucepan. Once the water is boiling, add the polenta in a steady stream, stirring continuously to prevent lumps forming. Reduce the heat to very low and simmer, stirring regularly, for about 20–25 minutes, or until the polenta starts to come away from the side of the pan.

Stir the Parmesan into the polenta and season with salt and pepper. Spoon the polenta into the baking tray, smooth the top with the back of a wet spoon and leave for 1 hour, or until set.

Once the polenta has set, carefully tip it out onto a board and cut into 24 x 5 cm squares, then cut each square into two triangles. Chargrill the polenta in batches on a preheated chargrill pan for 2–3 minutes on each side, or until warmed through.

Spread each triangle with 1 teaspoon of the pesto, top with a slice of bocconcini and a tomato quarter. Season and grill for 1–2 minutes, or until the cheese is just starting to melt. Garnish with basil and serve immediately.

Makes 48

Prawn and pesto pizza

Pizza dough
7 g sachet dried yeast
1/2 teaspoon caster sugar
2 cups (250 g) plain flour
1 tablespoon olive oil

2 tablespoons olive oil
1 teaspoon finely chopped fresh basil
1 clove garlic, crushed
24 cooked medium prawns, peeled
  and deveined
1/4 cup (60 g) ready-made pesto
24 small fresh basil leaves
24 pine nuts

Combine the yeast, sugar and 3/4 cup (185 ml) warm water, cover and leave for 10 minutes, or until frothy. If it hasn't foamed after 10 minutes, discard and start again.

Sift the flour and 1/2 teaspoon salt and make a well. Add the yeast mixture and the oil. Mix with a flat-bladed knife, using a cutting action, until a dough forms. Turn onto a floured surface and knead for 10 minutes, or until smooth. Transfer to an oiled bowl, cover with plastic wrap and leave for 45 minutes, or until doubled in size. Meanwhile, combine the oil, basil, garlic and prawns in a non-metallic bowl. Cover with plastic wrap and refrigerate for 30 minutes.

Preheat the oven to very hot 230°C (450°F/Gas 8). Punch down the dough, then knead for 8 minutes, or until elastic. Divide into 24 balls and roll each ball into a circle 4 mm thick and 4.5 cm in diameter. Prick the surfaces with a fork and brush with oil.

Place the bases on a lightly greased baking tray. Spread 1/2 teaspoon of pesto over each base, leaving a narrow border. Put a prawn, basil leaf and pine nut on each pizza and bake for 8–10 minutes.

Makes 24

Satay chicken sticks

8 large chicken tenderloins, trimmed
and sliced into thirds lengthways
1 clove garlic, crushed
3 teaspoons fish sauce
2 teaspoons grated fresh ginger
24 fresh kaffir lime leaves
lime quarters, to serve

Satay sauce
2 teaspoons peanut oil
4 red Asian shallots, finely chopped
2 cloves garlic, chopped
2 teaspoons grated fresh ginger
2 small red chillies, finely chopped
200 ml coconut milk
1/2 cup (125 g) crunchy peanut butter
2 tablespoons grated palm sugar or
soft brown sugar
2 tablespoons lime juice
1 1/2 tablespoons fish sauce
2 teaspoons soy sauce
1 fresh kaffir lime leaf

Combine the chicken, garlic, fish
sauce and ginger. Cover, then
refrigerate for 1 hour.

To make the sauce, heat the oil in a
saucepan over medium heat. Add the
shallots, garlic, ginger and chilli and
cook for 5 minutes, or until golden.
Add the rest of the ingredients,
reduce the heat and simmer for
10 minutes, or until thick.

Thread a lime leaf and a chicken strip
onto each skewer, then cook on a hot
barbecue hotplate or chargrill pan for
3–4 minutes. Serve with satay sauce
and lime wedges.

Makes 24

Sweet potato and lentil pastry pouches

2 tablespoons olive oil
1 large leek, finely chopped
2 cloves garlic, crushed
125 g button mushrooms, roughly
  chopped
2 teaspoons ground cumin
2 teaspoons ground coriander
1/2 cup (95 g) brown or green lentils
1/2 cup (125 g) red lentils
2 cups (500 ml) vegetable stock
300 g sweet potato, diced
4 tablespoons finely chopped fresh
  coriander leaves
8 sheets ready-rolled puff pastry
1 egg, lightly beaten
1/2 leek, extra, cut into 5 mm wide
  strips
200 g plain yoghurt
2 tablespoons grated Lebanese
  cucumber
1/2 teaspoon soft brown sugar

Preheat the oven to moderately hot 200°C (400°F/Gas 6). Heat the oil in a saucepan over medium heat and cook the leek for 2–3 minutes, or until soft. Add the garlic, mushrooms, cumin and ground coriander and cook for 1 minute, or until fragrant.

Add the combined lentils and stock and bring to the boil. Reduce the heat and simmer for 20–25 minutes, or until the lentils are cooked through, stirring occasionally. Add the sweet potato in the last 5 minutes.

Transfer to a bowl and stir in the coriander. Season to taste. Cool.

Cut the pastry sheets into four even squares. Place 1 1/2 tablespoons of filling into the centre of each square and bring the edges together to form a pouch. Pinch together, then tie each pouch with string. Lightly brush with egg and place on lined baking trays. Bake for 20–25 minutes, or until the pastry is puffed and golden.

Soak the leek strips in boiling water for 30 seconds. Remove the string and re-tie with a piece of blanched leek. Put the yoghurt, cucumber and sugar in a bowl and mix together well. Serve with the pastry pouches.

Makes 32

Thai fish cakes with dipping sauce

500 g firm white fish fillets, skin
  removed
1½ tablespoons red curry paste
¼ cup (60 g) sugar
¼ cup (60 ml) fish sauce
1 egg
100 g snake beans, thinly sliced
10 fresh kaffir lime leaves, finely
  chopped
oil, for deep-frying

Dipping sauce
½ cup (125 g) sugar
¼ cup (60 ml) white vinegar
1 tablespoon fish sauce
1 small fresh red chilli, chopped
2 tablespoons finely chopped carrot
2 tablespoons peeled, seeded and
  finely chopped cucumber
1 tablespoon roasted peanuts,
  chopped

Place the fish in a food processor
and process until smooth. Add the
curry paste, sugar, fish sauce and
egg. Process for another 10 seconds,
or until combined. Stir in the beans
and chopped lime leaves.

Shape the mixture into walnut-size
balls, then flatten them into patties.

Fill a wok one-third full of oil and heat
to 180°C (350°F), or until a cube of
bread dropped into the oil browns
in 15 seconds. Cook in batches for
3–5 minutes, turning occasionally.
Drain on crumpled paper towels.

To make the dipping sauce, place the
sugar, vinegar, fish sauce, chilli and
½ cup (125 ml) water in a saucepan.
Simmer for 5 minutes, or until
thickened slightly. Cool. Stir in
the chopped carrot, cucumber and
peanuts. Serve the dipping sauce
with the fish cakes.

Makes 24

Think ahead: The fish cakes can
be prepared, shaped and placed
on baking trays lined with plastic wrap
and kept in the fridge a day ahead.
Cook them just before serving.

Burgundy beef pies

Filling
2 tablespoons olive oil
500 g diced lean beef (topside)
1 onion, finely chopped
50 g pancetta, finely chopped
2 cloves garlic, crushed
1 tablespoon tomato paste (purée)
1 cup (250 ml) red wine
½ cup (125 ml) beef stock
1 teaspoon dried Italian herbs
½ cup (125 g) puréed tomatoes

750 g ready-made shortcrust pastry
1 egg, lightly beaten

Heat half the oil in a large saucepan and cook the beef in batches over high heat for 5 minutes, or until browned. Remove the meat and set aside. Add the remaining oil and cook the onion, pancetta and garlic for 3–4 minutes, or until soft. Return the meat to the pan, stir in the rest of the ingredients, cover and simmer for 50–60 minutes, or until the meat is tender. Remove the lid and cook for a further 30 minutes, or until the sauce is reduced. Allow to cool.

Preheat the oven to moderate 180°C (350°F/Gas 4) and put a baking tray in the oven. Grease 24 mini muffin holes. Roll the pastry thinly and cut out 24 rounds with a 7 cm cutter. Repeat with a 5.5 cm cutter. Put one of the larger rounds in each muffin hole and fill with the cooled filling. Dampen the edges of the small rounds and place them on top of the filling to seal the pies. Brush with egg. Put the tin on the hot baking tray and cook for 25 minutes, or until golden. Cool slightly, then remove from the tin.

Makes 24

Vegetable pakoras with minted yoghurt sauce

1 cup (250 g) plain yoghurt
1 cup (20 g) fresh mint
2 tablespoons coriander seeds
1 tablespoon cumin seeds
1½ cups (165 g) besan (chickpea flour) (see Note)
1½ teaspoons chilli powder
1 teaspoon ground turmeric
3 tablespoons finely chopped fresh coriander
1 teaspoon oil
400 g cauliflower florets, cut into 1 cm pieces
1 small onion, thinly sliced
1 cup (135 g) grated zucchini (courgette)
1 clove garlic, crushed
oil, for deep-frying
lemon wedges, to serve

To make the dipping sauce, put the yoghurt and mint in a food processor and pulse for 10–20 seconds, or until the mint is thoroughly chopped.

Toast the coriander and cumin seeds in a dry frying pan over low heat for 2–3 minutes, or until fragrant. Cool slightly, then grind to a powder. Transfer to a large bowl and add the besan, chilli powder, turmeric, fresh coriander and 1 teaspoon salt. Mix well, stir in the oil, then gradually add ⅔ cup (170 ml) warm water and stir until a smooth, thick paste forms. Mix the cauliflower, onion, zucchini and garlic into the batter.

Fill a deep heavy-based saucepan one-third full of oil and heat to 180°C (350°F), or until a cube of bread browns in 15 seconds. Carefully add 1 tablespoon of the batter to the oil, then repeat until you are cooking five pakoras at one time. Cook each batch for 2 minutes each side, or until golden. Drain on paper towels. Sprinkle with salt and repeat with the remaining mixture. Serve hot with yoghurt sauce and lemon wedges.

Makes 40

Note: Besan flour is available from health food stores.

Mini spicy pork quesadillas

2¾ tablespoons olive oil
½ teaspoon ground oregano
1 teaspoon ground cumin
½ teaspoon garlic salt
½ teaspoon cayenne pepper
350 g pork mince
2–3 chopped jalapeño chillies in brine
¼ cup (30 g) pitted black olives, sliced
⅓ cup (55 g) green olives stuffed with red pimentos, sliced
2 tablespoons chopped fresh coriander leaves
12 x 16 cm flour tortillas
½ cup (60 g) grated mild Cheddar
½ cup (75 g) grated mozzarella
fresh coriander sprigs, to garnish

To make the spicy pork mince, heat 1½ tablespoons of the olive oil in a large frying pan; when hot add the oregano, cumin, garlic salt and cayenne pepper and cook for 30 seconds. Add the pork mince and cook over high heat for 10 minutes, before incorporating the chillies and all the olives. Cook for another 5 minutes, then stir in the chopped coriander. Remove from the heat and allow to cool.

Cut each tortilla in half. Place 1 tablespoon of filling on one half of each half. Mix the cheeses together, then put 1 tablespoon of the grated cheese on top of the spicy pork mince. Turn the flap of tortilla over the filling and press down firmly.

Heat 2 teaspoons of the remaining oil in a non-stick frying pan over high heat and cook the quesadillas in batches of six for 3–4 minutes each side, or until golden. Add a teaspoon of oil to the pan after each batch. Garnish with coriander sprigs.

Makes 24

Variation: For a very simple vegetarian filling, simply sprinkle each half tortilla with 1 tablespoon chopped tomato, chilli, olives and coriander, then the cheese; fold over and cook as for the pork quesadillas.

Prawn potstickers

Dipping sauce
1/4 cup (60 ml) soy sauce
1 spring onion, thinly sliced
1 clove garlic, crushed
1/4 teaspoon finely chopped fresh
  ginger
1/4 teaspoon sesame oil

500 g raw medium prawns
40 g Chinese cabbage, finely
  shredded
40 g drained water chestnuts, finely
  chopped
1 tablespoon finely chopped fresh
  coriander leaves
24 round gow gee wrappers
  (see Note)
1 tablespoon vegetable oil
1/2 cup (125 ml) chicken stock

To make the dipping sauce, mix together all the ingredients in a small bowl.

Peel and devein the prawns, then finely chop. Combine the prawn meat, cabbage, water chestnuts and coriander.

Lay all the gow gee wrappers out on a work surface and put one heaped teaspoon of the prawn filling in the centre of each. Moisten the edges with water and draw together into the shape of a moneybag, pressing the edges together firmly to seal.

Heat the oil in a large frying pan and add the potstickers. Cook in batches over medium heat for 2 minutes, or until just brown on the bottom. Add the stock, then quickly cover with a lid as it will spit. Steam for 2–3 minutes, taking care that all the stock does not evaporate and the potstickers do not burn. Serve immediately with the dipping sauce.

Makes 24

Note: Gow gee wrappers are rolled out round pieces of dough made from wheat flour and water. They are available from Asian food stores.

Mediterranean twists

2 tablespoons olive oil
2 onions, thinly sliced
1/3 cup (80 ml) dry white wine
3 teaspoons sugar
1 cup (30 g) chopped fresh flat-leaf
  parsley
8 anchovies, drained and finely
  chopped
1 cup (130 g) coarsely grated Gruyère
6 sheets filo pastry
60 g unsalted butter, melted

Preheat the oven to hot 220°C (425°F/Gas 7) and warm a baking tray. Heat the oil in a frying pan and cook the onion over low heat for 5 minutes. Add the wine and sugar, and cook for 10–15 minutes, or until the onion is golden. Remove from the heat and cool.

Combine the parsley with the anchovies, cheese and cooled onion.

Keeping the filo covered while you work, take one sheet, brush lightly with the butter, cover with another sheet and repeat until you have three buttered sheets. Spread the parsley mixture over the pastry and top with the remaining three sheets, buttering each layer as before. Press down firmly, then cut the pastry in half widthways, then cut each half into strips 1.5–2 cm wide. Brush with butter, then gently twist each strip. Lightly season with black pepper, place on a baking tray and bake for 10–15 minutes, or until golden.

Makes 24

Think ahead: Make the twists up to 2 days before the party and store them in an airtight container. To refresh them, warm them in a moderate 180°C (350°F/Gas 4) oven for 10 minutes before serving.

Mini steak sandwiches

100 ml olive oil
1 onion, thinly sliced
¾ cup (15 g) fresh parsley
10 large fresh basil leaves
20 fresh mint leaves
1 clove garlic, crushed
1 tablespoon Dijon mustard
1 tablespoon capers
2 anchovy fillets
400 g fillet steak, about 1 cm thick
1 baguette, cut into 40 x 5 mm slices

Heat 2 tablespoons of oil in a frying pan and cook the onion over low heat for 25 minutes, or until caramelised.

To make the salsa verde, place the parsley, basil, mint, garlic, mustard, capers, anchovies and the remaining oil in a food processor and pulse to a thick paste. Season.

Cut out 20 rounds from the steak with a 2.5 cm cutter. Season, then sear on a lightly oiled chargrill pan on both sides for 1–2 minutes, or until cooked to your liking. Put a little of the onion on 20 rounds of bread, top with a piece of steak and a dollop of salsa verde, then top with the remaining bread. Serve warm.

Makes 20

Gyoza

300 g pork mince
250 g finely shredded and lightly
    blanched Chinese cabbage with the
    excess water squeezed out
60 g fresh Chinese chives, chopped
1 tablespoon finely chopped fresh
    ginger
1/4 cup (60 ml) soy sauce
1 tablespoon rice wine
1 teaspoon sugar
45 gow gee wrappers
2 teaspoons oil

Dipping sauce
2 tablespoons soy sauce
1 tablespoon black Chinese vinegar
1 teaspoon sesame oil
1/2 teaspoon chilli oil

Combine the pork mince, Chinese cabbage, Chinese chives and ginger in a bowl. Add the soy sauce, rice wine, sugar and 1 teaspoon salt and mix together very well.

Place a gow gee wrapper flat in the palm of your hand, then place 2 teaspoons of the filling mixture into the centre of the wrapper. With wet fingers, bring the sides together to form a half-moon shape and pinch the seam firmly to seal it in a pleat.

Press one side of the dumplings onto a flat surface to create a flat bottom; this will make the dumplings easier to pan-fry.

Heat the oil in a frying pan over medium–high heat. Add the gyoza to the pan in batches and cook for 1–2 minutes on the flat side, without moving, so that the gyoza become brown and crisp on that side. Transfer to a plate. Return the gyoza to the pan in batches, then gradually add 100 ml water to the pan and cover. Steam for 5 minutes. Empty the pan and wipe it dry between batches.

To make the dipping sauce, combine all the ingredients in a small bowl. Serve with the gyoza.

Makes 45

Honey prawns

16 raw large prawns
cornflour, for dusting
oil, for deep-frying
3 egg whites, lightly beaten
2 tablespoons cornflour, extra
2 tablespoons oil, extra
¼ cup (90 g) honey
2 tablespoons sesame seeds, toasted

Peel and devein the prawns, leaving the tails intact. Pat them dry and lightly dust with the cornflour, shaking off any excess. Fill a large heavy-based saucepan or wok one-third full of oil and heat to 180°C (350°F), or until a cube of bread dropped in the oil browns in 15 seconds.

Beat the egg whites in a clean dry bowl until soft peaks form. Add the extra cornflour and some salt and gently whisk until combined and smooth. Using the tail as a handle, dip the prawns in the batter, then slowly lower them into the oil. Cook in batches for 3–4 minutes, or until crisp and golden and the prawns are cooked. Remove with a slotted spoon, then drain on crumpled paper towels and keep warm.

Heat the extra oil and honey in a saucepan over medium heat for 2–3 minutes, or until bubbling. Place the prawns on a serving plate and pour on the honey sauce. Sprinkle with the sesame seeds and serve immediately with steamed rice.

Makes 16

Grilled figs in prosciutto

50 g unsalted butter
2 tablespoons orange juice
6 small–medium fresh figs
6 long thin slices of prosciutto,
  trimmed of excess fat
24 sage leaves

Place the butter in a small heavy-based saucepan. Melt over low heat, then cook the butter for 8–10 minutes, or until the froth subsides and the milk solids appear as brown specks on the bottom of the saucepan. Strain the butter into a clean bowl by pouring it through a strainer lined with a clean tea towel or paper towel. Stir the orange juice into the strained butter.

Gently slice the figs lengthways into quarters. Cut each slice of prosciutto into four even strips. Sit a sage leaf on each fig segment, then wrap a piece of prosciutto around the middle with the ends tucked under the bottom of the fig. Arrange the figs, cut-side-up, on a baking tray and brush lightly with the butter mixture.

Move the grill tray to its lowest position, then preheat the grill to hot. Place the baking tray of figs on the grill tray and grill the figs for 1–1½ minutes, or until the prosciutto becomes slightly crispy. Serve hot or at room temperature. If you are serving the figs hot, provide serviettes to avoid burnt fingers.

Makes 24

Think ahead: The figs can be wrapped up to 6 hours in advance and covered in plastic wrap. Cook them just before serving.

Zucchini and haloumi fritters

300 g zucchini (courgette)
4 spring onions, thinly sliced
200 g haloumi cheese, coarsely
  grated
1/4 cup (30 g) plain flour
2 eggs
1 tablespoon chopped fresh dill,
  plus sprigs, to garnish
1/4 cup (60 ml) oil
1 lemon, cut into very thin slices,
  seeds removed
1/3 cup (90 g) thick Greek-style
  yoghurt

Coarsely grate the zucchini and squeeze out as much liquid as possible in your hands or in a clean tea towel. Combine the zucchini with the spring onion, haloumi, flour, eggs and dill. Season well with salt and cracked black pepper.

Heat the oil in a large heavy-based frying pan. Form fritters (using heaped teaspoons of the mixture) and cook in batches for 2 minutes each side, or until golden and firm. Drain on crumpled paper towels.

Cut each slice of lemon into quarters or eighths, depending on the size, to make small triangles.

Top each fritter with 1/2 teaspoon yoghurt, a piece of lemon and a small sprig of dill.

Makes 45

Note: The fritters are best prepared and cooked as close to the serving time as possible or the haloumi tends to go a little tough.

Prawn toasts

Dipping sauce
1/2 cup (125 ml) tomato sauce
2 cloves garlic, crushed
2 small red chillies, seeded and finely
  chopped
2 tablespoons hoisin sauce
2 teaspoons Worcestershire sauce

350 g raw medium prawns
1 clove garlic
75 g canned water chestnuts, drained
1 tablespoon chopped fresh coriander
2 cm x 2 cm piece fresh ginger,
  roughly chopped
2 eggs, separated
1/4 teaspoon white pepper
12 slices white bread, crusts removed
1 cup (155 g) sesame seeds
oil, for deep-frying

To make the dipping sauce, combine all the ingredients in a small bowl.

Peel the prawns and gently pull out the dark vein from each prawn back, starting at the head end. Put the prawns in a food processor with the garlic, water chestnuts, coriander, ginger, egg whites, pepper and 1/4 teaspoon salt and process for 20–30 seconds, or until smooth.

Brush the top of each slice of bread with lightly beaten egg yolk, then spread evenly with the prawn mixture. Sprinkle generously with sesame seeds. Cut each slice of bread into three even strips.

Fill a large heavy-based saucepan one-third full of oil and heat to 180°C (350°F), or until a cube of bread browns in 15 seconds. Deep-fry the toasts in batches for 10–15 seconds, or until golden and crisp. Start with the prawn mixture face down, then turn halfway. Remove the toasts from the oil with tongs or a slotted spoon and drain on crumpled paper towels. Serve with the dipping sauce.

Makes 36

Think ahead: The uncooked prawn toasts can be frozen for up to 1 month. Allow them to thaw slightly before deep-frying as instructed.

Deep-fried chicken balls

50 g dried rice vermicelli
500 g chicken mince
3 cloves garlic, finely chopped
1 tablespoon chopped fresh ginger
1 red chilli, seeded and finely
  chopped
1 egg, lightly beaten
2 spring onions, finely sliced
1/3 cup (20 g) chopped fresh coriander
  leaves
1/3 cup (40 g) plain flour
1/3 cup (60 g) finely chopped water
  chestnuts
oil, for deep-frying

Dipping sauce
1/2 cup (125 ml) sweet chilli sauce
1/2 cup (125 ml) soy sauce
1 tablespoon Chinese rice wine

Cover the vermicelli with boiling water
and soak for 6–7 minutes. Drain, then
cut into short lengths.

Combine the mince, garlic, ginger,
chilli, egg, spring onion, coriander,
flour and water chestnuts in a large
bowl. Mix in the vermicelli and season
with salt. Refrigerate for 30 minutes.
Roll heaped tablespoons of mixture
into balls.

Fill a wok or deep saucepan one-third
full with oil and heat to 180°C (350°F),
or until a cube of bread browns in
15 seconds. Deep-fry the balls in
batches for 2 minutes, or until golden
brown and cooked through. Drain.

To make the dipping sauce, mix the
sweet chilli sauce, soy sauce and rice
wine. Serve with the hot chicken balls.

Makes about 30

Mushroom ragout tartlets

Basic pastry cases
2 cups (250 g) plain flour
125 g chilled butter, chopped
1 egg

50 g butter
4 spring onions, chopped
2 cloves garlic, chopped
150 g small Swiss brown or shiitake
   mushrooms, thinly sliced
100 g oyster mushrooms, cut into
   eighths
50 g enoki mushrooms, trimmed,
   pulled apart and sliced lengthways
3 teaspoons plain flour
2 tablespoons chicken stock or water
2 tablespoons sake
1/3 cup (80 ml) thick (double) cream
snow pea sprouts, stalks removed

Preheat the oven to moderately hot
200°C (400°F/Gas 6). Lightly grease
30 mini muffin holes. Sift the flour and
rub the butter in with your fingertips
until the mixture resembles fine
breadcrumbs. Make a well in the
centre, add the egg and mix with
a flat-bladed knife, using a cutting
action until it comes together in
beads. If the dough seems too dry,
add a little cold water. Press the
dough into a ball on a lightly floured
surface, then wrap it in plastic wrap
and refrigerate for 30 minutes.

Roll out the dough between sheets of
baking paper to 2 mm thick. Cut out
30 rounds with a 6 cm cutter. Press a
round into each hole. Prick the bases
with a fork and bake for 8 minutes,
or until golden. If they puff up, use
a clean cloth to press back. Cool.

Melt the butter in a frying pan over
medium heat, add the spring onion
and garlic and cook for 1 minute. Add
the mushrooms and cook, stirring, for
3–4 minutes, or until soft. Add the
flour and stir for another minute. Pour
in the stock and sake and stir for
1 minute, or until evaporated, then
add the cream and cook for 1 minute,
or until thickened. Season. Spoon into
the prepared pastry cases and top
each one with a snow pea sprout leaf.

Makes 30

Tomato and basil bruschetta

1 loaf Italian bread
1 large clove garlic, peeled
extra virgin olive oil, to drizzle
3 large (400 g) vine-ripened tomatoes,
    cut into 1 cm pieces
1/4 cup (60 ml) extra virgin olive oil
1/3 cup (10 g) fresh basil, torn into
    small pieces

Preheat the oven to moderately hot
200°C (400°F/Gas 6). Slice the loaf
of bread on the diagonal into twelve
1 cm thick slices. Lay the bread slices
out in a single layer on a baking tray
and bake for 10–12 minutes, or until
they are lightly golden. Remove from
the oven and rub the garlic clove over
one side of each slice of toast. Lightly
drizzle each slice with extra virgin
olive oil, then cut them in half again
so that each piece is easily handled
by your guests.

Place the tomato slices in a bowl
with the extra virgin olive oil and
torn basil. Season with salt and
cracked black pepper and toss until
well combined. Spoon the mixture
onto the prepared bruschetta slices
and serve immediately.

Makes 24

Note: Bruschetta are best made at
the last moment to prevent the bread
drying out or the topping from making
the bread soggy.
Variation: A simple alternative to
topping is to lightly sprinkle the
prepared bruschetta with some
fresh or dried chopped herbs.

Scallops with goat's cheese and crispy prosciutto

4 thin slices prosciutto
16 scallops on shells, roe and beards removed
2–3 tablespoons extra virgin olive oil
1 tablespoon chopped fresh flat-leaf parsley
½ teaspoon sea salt flakes
100 g goat's cheese, crumbled
2 tablespoons good-quality aged balsamic vinegar

Cook the prosciutto under a hot grill until crisp, then drain on paper towels and break into small pieces.

Place the scallops on two baking trays. Combine the oil and parsley in a small bowl and season with sea salt and cracked black pepper. Brush the scallops with the oil mixture.

Cook the scallops in batches under a hot grill for 2–3 minutes, or until they are tender.

Top the scallops with the goat's cheese, prosciutto and a drizzle of balsamic vinegar.

Carefully transfer the scallops from the trays to serving plates lined with rock salt—the shells will be very hot. Serve with small cocktail forks to avoid messy fingers.

Makes 16

Corn pancakes

6 fresh corn cobs or 325 g can corn
  kernels, drained
4 spring onions, finely chopped
1 clove garlic, crushed
1 teaspoon curry powder
2 tablespoons self-raising flour
1 teaspoon soy sauce
1 egg
oil, for shallow-frying

If using fresh corn, remove the kernels with a sharp knife. Combine the corn, spring onion, garlic, curry powder, flour, soy sauce and egg, mashing lightly with a potato masher. Cover with plastic wrap and chill for 1 hour.

Heat 4 tablespoons of oil in a frying pan. Drop tablespoons of the corn mixture into the pan—avoid overcrowding. Cook over medium heat for 2–3 minutes, on each side, or until golden brown—turn carefully to prevent the pancakes breaking. Remove from the pan and drain on paper towels. Repeat with the remaining mixture.

Delicious served with sweet chilli sauce, if desired.

Makes 12

Sigara Boregi

500 g English spinach
1 tablespoon olive oil
4 cloves garlic, crushed
200 g French shallots, finely chopped
½ cup (75 g) crumbled feta cheese
1 egg, lightly beaten
3 tablespoons chopped fresh flat-leaf
  parsley
¼ teaspoon finely grated lemon zest
¼ teaspoon paprika
pinch of nutmeg
6 sheets filo pastry
125 g butter, melted
light olive oil, for deep-frying

Wash the spinach, leaving it quite wet. Place in a saucepan, cover and cook over low heat until just wilted. Tip the spinach into a colander and press out the liquid with a wooden spoon. When cool, squeeze dry.

Heat the oil in a frying pan, and cook the garlic and shallots for 2 minutes, or until soft but not browned. Transfer to a bowl and add the feta cheese, egg, parsley, spinach and lemon zest. Season with the paprika, nutmeg and salt and pepper, and mix well.

Brush a sheet of filo with melted butter, then fold it in half lengthways. It should measure about 32 x 12 cm. Cut in half widthways. Brush with butter, place 1 heaped tablespoon of filling at one end of each piece and spread to within 1 cm of each side. Fold in the sides to cover the edges of the filling, continuing the folds right up the length of the pastry. Brush with melted butter, then roll up tightly. Brush the outside with butter and seal. Cover with a damp tea towel while you prepare the rest.

Heat the light olive oil in a deep frying pan to 180°C (350°F), or until a cube of bread browns in 15 seconds. Deep-fry in batches until golden. Serve warm or at room temperature.

Makes 12

Crunchy Thai chicken and peanut cakes

3 teaspoons grated palm sugar or
  soft brown sugar
1 tablespoon fish sauce
350 g chicken mince
3/4 cup (120 g) toasted peanuts,
  chopped
1/2 cup (40 g) fresh breadcrumbs
1 tablespoon red Thai curry paste
1 tablespoon lime juice
3 fresh kaffir lime leaves, very finely
  shredded
2 tablespoons sweet chilli sauce
2 tablespoons chopped fresh
  coriander
1/2 cup (125 ml) oil
1 banana leaf, cut into 24 x 5 cm
  square pieces
sweet chilli sauce, extra, to serve

Dissolve the sugar in the fish sauce, then place in a bowl with the chicken mince, peanuts, breadcrumbs, curry paste, lime juice, lime leaves, sweet chilli sauce and coriander. Mix well. Divide the mixture into 24 small balls—they will be quite soft. Flatten the balls into discs about 1.5 cm thick. Lay them in a single layer on a tray, cover with plastic wrap and refrigerate for 30 minutes.

Heat the oil in a heavy-based frying pan and cook the cakes in batches for 2–3 minutes each side, or until firm and golden. Drain on crumpled paper towels.

Place a chicken cake on each square of banana leaf and top with a dash of sweet chilli sauce. Secure with a toothpick for easier serving.

Makes 24

Think ahead: The uncooked Thai chicken cakes will keep frozen for up to 2 months or refrigerated in a single layer for 1 day.

Chargrilled vegetable skewers

24 bay leaves
12 button mushrooms, cut in half
1 yellow capsicum (pepper), cut into
 2 cm pieces
1 red capsicum, (pepper) cut into
 2 cm pieces
1 zucchini (courgette), cut into 2 cm
 pieces
1 small red onion, cut into 2 cm
 pieces
½ cup (125 ml) olive oil
2 tablespoons lemon juice
1 clove garlic, crushed
2 teaspoons fresh thyme

Concassé
1 tablespoon olive oil
1 small onion, finely chopped
1 clove garlic, crushed
425 g can chopped tomatoes
4 tablespoons torn fresh basil

Thread 24 skewers in the following order: bay leaf, mushroom, yellow capsicum, red capsicum, zucchini and onion, then put in a large flat non-metallic dish and season with salt and cracked black pepper.

Place the oil, lemon juice, garlic and thyme in a small bowl and mix together. Pour over the skewers and marinate for 20 minutes.

Meanwhile, to make the concassé, heat the oil in a small saucepan, add the onion and cook for 5 minutes, or until soft. Add the garlic and cook for 30 seconds, then add the tomato. Simmer for 10–15 minutes over medium heat, then add the basil. Cook the skewers on a hot barbecue hotplate or chargrill pan for 3 minutes each side, or until golden, brushing occasionally with the marinade. Serve with the concassé.

Makes 24

Salt cod fritters

500 g salt cod
1 large potato (200 g), unpeeled
2 tablespoons milk
¼ cup (60 ml) olive oil
1 small onion, finely chopped
2 cloves garlic, crushed
¼ cup (30 g) self-raising flour
2 eggs, separated
1 tablespoon finely chopped fresh
  flat-leaf parsley
oil, for deep-frying

Soak the cod in cold water for 24 hours, changing the water at least three times. Boil the potato for 20 minutes, or until soft. Drain. When cool enough to handle, peel and mash with the milk and 2 tablespoons of the olive oil. Drain the cod, cut into pieces and place in a saucepan. Cover with cold water, bring to the boil over high heat, then simmer for 10 minutes, or until soft. Drain. When cool enough to handle, remove the skin and any bones. Mash with a fork until flaky. (You should have 200 g of flesh.)

Heat the remaining olive oil in a frying pan. Cook the onion over medium heat for 5 minutes, or until softened and browning. Add the garlic and cook for 1 minute. Remove from the heat.

Combine the potato, cod, onion mixture, flour, egg yolks and parsley, and season with cracked black pepper. Whisk the egg whites until stiff then fold into the mixture.

Fill a large heavy-based saucepan one-third full with oil and heat to 190°C (375°F), or until a cube of bread browns in 10 seconds. Drop level tablespoons of the mixture into the oil and cook for 2 minutes, or until puffed and golden. Drain on crumpled paper towels and serve.

Makes 28

Prawns in Chinese pancakes

24 raw medium prawns, peeled and deveined
1/3 cup (80 ml) Chinese rice wine or dry sherry
2 tablespoons soy sauce
2 teaspoons sesame oil
2 tablespoons vegetable oil
4 cloves garlic, finely chopped
1 cm x 4 cm piece fresh ginger, peeled and finely shredded
120–160 ml Chinese plum sauce
2 teaspoons chilli sauce
2 spring onions, finely chopped
24 Chinese pancakes (see Note)
1 small Lebanese cucumber, peeled, seeded and cut into thin 5 cm long strips
12 garlic chives, cut into 5 cm lengths

Place the prawns in a non-metallic bowl with the rice wine, soy sauce and sesame oil and marinate for at least 10 minutes.

Heat a wok over high heat, add the vegetable oil and swirl to coat. Add the garlic and ginger and sauté for 1–2 minutes. Use a slotted spoon or tongs to remove the prawns from the marinade and add them to the wok. Reserve the marinade. Stir the prawns for 2 minutes, or until they start to turn pink, then add the plum sauce, chilli sauce and the reserved marinade. Stir-fry for 2–3 minutes, or until the prawns are cooked, curled and slightly glazed. Remove from the heat and stir in the spring onion.

Place the pancakes in a non-stick frying pan over medium heat for 1 minute, or until warm.

To assemble, put a prawn, a few slices of cucumber and a few chive pieces on each pancake, spoon on some sauce, then fold over. Serve immediately.

Makes 24

Note: Buy the pancakes, traditionally used for Peking duck, in the freezer of Asian food stores.

Spring rolls

50 g mung bean vermicelli
1 tablespoon oil
2 large cloves garlic, crushed
2 tablespoons grated fresh ginger
6 spring onions, chopped
4 fresh coriander roots, finely
  chopped
200 g peeled raw prawns, minced
200 g pork mince
1 carrot (125 g), grated
3 tablespoons finely chopped fresh
  coriander leaves
2 tablespoons sweet chilli sauce
1 tablespoon fish sauce
2 tablespoons soy sauce
30 small spring roll wrappers
1 egg white, lightly beaten
oil, extra, for deep-frying

Soak the vermicelli in warm water
for 5 minutes. Drain and cut into
short lengths.

Heat the oil in a large saucepan over
medium heat. Add the garlic, ginger,
spring onion and coriander root. Cook
for 1–2 minutes, or until soft. Add the
prawn and pork mince and cook, until
cooked through, breaking up the
lumps. Stir in the vermicelli, carrot and
coriander leaves. Cook for 1 minute.
Add the sweet chilli, fish and soy
sauces and cook for 2 minutes, or
until dry. Cool.

Place a tablespoon of the mixture
along the centre of each spring roll
wrapper. Brush the edge with egg
white and roll up, tucking in the ends
as you go. Cover to prevent drying.

Fill a deep heavy-based saucepan
one-third full of oil and heat to 190°C
(375°F), or until a cube of bread
browns in 10 seconds. Cook the
rolls in batches for 30–60 seconds,
or until golden. Drain.

Makes 30

Sesame and wasabi-crusted tuna cubes

Ginger and soy dipping sauce
2 cm x 2 cm piece fresh ginger,
  cut into julienne strips
2 tablespoons Japanese soy sauce
2 tablespoons mirin
1 teaspoon wasabi paste
¼ teaspoon sesame oil

Tuna cubes
600 g fresh tuna steaks
1 teaspoon wasabi powder
⅓ cup (50 g) black sesame seeds
¼ cup (60 ml) oil

To make the dipping sauce, combine the ginger, Japanese soy sauce, mirin, wasabi paste and sesame oil.

Cut the tuna into 2 cm cubes using a very sharp knife. Toss with the combined wasabi powder and black sesame seeds until evenly coated.

Heat a wok over high heat, add half the oil and swirl to coat. Add half the tuna and cook, tossing gently, for 1–2 minutes, or until lightly golden on the outside but still pink in the middle. Drain on crumpled paper towels and repeat with the remaining oil and tuna. Arrange on a platter with dipping sauce in the centre and serve with toothpicks so that your guests can pick up the cubes.

Makes about 40

Think ahead: The dipping sauce will keep in the refrigerator for up to 1 week, but the tuna is best if cooked no more than 3 hours in advance. Variation: Try a chilli and lime dipping sauce instead of the ginger and soy one above. Dissolve 2 tablespoons grated palm sugar or soft brown sugar in 2 tablespoons lime juice. Add 1 tablespoon fish sauce and 1 seeded and chopped fresh red bird's eye chilli. Mix together well. This sauce will keep in the refrigerator for 2–3 days.

Pesto palmiers

1 cup (50 g) fresh basil leaves
1 clove garlic, crushed
¼ cup (25 g) grated Parmesan
1 tablespoon pine nuts, toasted
2 tablespoons olive oil
4 sheets ready-rolled puff pastry,
  thawed

Preheat the oven to hot 220°C (425°F/Gas 7). Roughly chop the basil leaves in a food processor with the garlic, Parmesan and pine nuts. With the motor running, gradually add the oil in a thin stream and process until the mixture is smooth.

Spread each pastry sheet with a quarter of the basil mixture. Roll up one side until you reach the middle then repeat with the other side. Place on a baking tray. Repeat with the remaining pastry and basil mixture. Freeze for 30 minutes.

Slice each roll into 1.5 cm slices. Curl each slice into a semi-circle and place on a lightly greased baking tray. Allow room for the palmiers to expand during cooking. Bake in batches for 15–20 minutes, or until golden brown.

Makes 60

Note: Palmiers are delicious bite-sized specially shaped pastry snacks which traditionally were sweet.
Variations: Spread with a prepared tapenade paste made with olives, capers, anchovies, oil and garlic, or with tahini, a sesame seed paste. Another simple version is to sprinkle just the grated Parmesan between the pastry layers.

Prawn, noodle and nori parcels

Dipping sauce
1/3 cup (80 ml) tonkatsu sauce or
  barbecue sauce
2 tablespoons lemon juice
1 tablespoon sake or mirin
1–2 teaspoons grated fresh ginger

250 g dried somen noodles
3 sheets nori (dried seaweed)
1/2 cup (60 g) plain flour
2 egg yolks
24 raw medium prawns, peeled and
  deveined with the tails intact
oil, for deep-frying

Combine the dipping sauce ingredients, adding the ginger to taste.

Using a sharp knife, cut the noodles to the same length as the prawns (from the head to the base of the tail). Keep the noodles in neat bundles. Cut the nori into 2.5 cm wide strips.

Sift the flour and make a well in the centre. Mix the egg yolks with 1/4 cup (60 ml) of water. Gradually add to the flour, whisking to make a smooth batter. Add another tablespoon of water if the mixture is too thick.

Dip a prawn in the batter, letting the excess run off. Roll the prawn lengthways in noodles to coat it with a single layer. Keep the noodles in place by rolling a nori strip around the centre of the prawn and securing it with a little batter. Repeat with the rest of the prawns.

Fill a deep heavy-based saucepan or deep-fryer one-third full of oil and heat to 180°C (350°F), or until a cube of bread browns in 15 seconds. Deep-fry 2–3 prawns at a time, for about 1–2 minutes, or until the prawns are cooked. Drain on crumpled paper towels and keep warm. Serve warm with the dipping sauce.

Makes 24

Dressed-up baby potatoes

24 even bite-sized new potatoes,
  washed and dried
⅓ cup (80 ml) olive oil
1 tablespoon drained capers, patted
  dry
1 rasher bacon
1 tablespoon cream
10 g butter
½ cup (125 g) sour cream
1 tablespoon chopped fresh chives
1 tablespoon red or black fish roe

Preheat the oven to moderate 180°C
(350°F/Gas 4). Line a baking tray with
baking paper. Place the potatoes in a
bowl and toss with half the olive oil.
Sprinkle with salt and black pepper,
then put on the baking tray and bake
for 40 minutes, or until cooked
through, rotating them 2–3 times
so that they brown evenly.

Meanwhile, heat the remaining oil in a
frying pan and cook the capers over
high heat, or until they open into small
flowers. Drain on paper towels. Cook
the bacon under a hot grill until crispy.
Cool, then finely chop.

Remove the potatoes from the oven.
When cool enough to handle, cut a
thin lid from each potato. Discard the
lids. Use a melon baller or small
teaspoon to scoop out the flesh from
the middle of the potatoes, leaving a
1 cm border. Put the potato flesh in a
bowl and mash thoroughly with the
cream, butter and salt and black
pepper. Spoon the mash back into
the potatoes.

Top each potato with a small dollop of
sour cream. Divide the potatoes into
four groups of six and use a separate
topping for each group: capers,
bacon, chives and fish roe.

Makes 24

Money bags

1 tablespoon peanut oil
4 red Asian shallots, finely chopped
2 cloves garlic, crushed
1 tablespoon grated fresh ginger
150 g chicken mince
150 g pork mince
¼ cup (40 g) roasted peanuts,
  chopped
3 tablespoons finely chopped
  fresh coriander leaves
3 teaspoons fish sauce
2 teaspoons soy sauce
2 teaspoons lime juice
2 teaspoons grated palm sugar or
  soft brown sugar
30 won ton wrappers
oil, for deep-frying
garlic chives, for tying

Dipping sauce
2 teaspoons sugar
½ cup (125 ml) vinegar
2 small fresh red chillies, seeded and
  chopped

Heat the oil in a frying pan over medium heat. Add the shallots, garlic and ginger and cook for 1–2 minutes, or until the shallots are soft. Add the mince and cook for 4 minutes, or until cooked, breaking up any lumps with a wooden spoon. Stir in the peanuts, coriander, fish sauce, soy sauce, lime juice and sugar and cook, stirring, for 1–2 minutes, or until mixed and reduced. Cool.

Form your thumb and index finger into a circle, and place a won ton wrapper on top. Place 2 teaspoons of the cooled mixture in the centre, then lightly brush the edges with water. Push the mixture down firmly with your free hand, tightening the circle of your thumb and index finger at the same time, encasing the mixture in the wrapper and forming a 'bag'. Trim.

Fill a deep heavy-based saucepan or deep-fryer one-third full of oil and heat to 190°C (375°F), or until a cube of bread browns in 10 seconds. Cook in batches for 30–60 seconds, or until golden. Drain. Tie the 'neck' of the money bags with the chives.

To make the dipping sauce, dissolve the sugar and 1 teaspoon salt in the vinegar. Add the chilli and mix. Serve with the dipping sauce.

Makes 30

Cocktail leek pies

60 g butter
2 tablespoons olive oil
1 onion, finely chopped
3 leeks, finely sliced
1 clove garlic, chopped
1 tablespoon plain flour
2 tablespoons sour cream
1 cup (100 g) grated Parmesan
1 teaspoon chopped fresh thyme
4 sheets frozen puff pastry, thawed
1 egg, lightly beaten

Heat the butter and oil in a large frying pan over medium heat. Add the onion and cook, stirring occasionally, for 2 minutes. Add the leek and garlic and cook for 5 minutes, or until the leek is softened and lightly coloured. Add the flour and stir into the mixture for 1 minute. Add the sour cream and stir until slightly thickened. Transfer to a bowl and add the Parmesan and thyme. Season with salt and cracked black pepper and allow to cool.

Preheat the oven to moderately hot 200°C (400°F/Gas 6). Place a lightly greased baking tray in the oven to heat. Using a 6 cm cutter, cut the pastry into 64 circles. Place 2 heaped teaspoons of filling on half the pastry circles, leaving a small border. Lightly brush the edges with egg, then place a pastry circle on top of each. Seal the edges well with a fork. Lightly brush the tops with egg. Place the pies on the heated tray and bake for 25 minutes, or until the pies are puffed and golden.

Makes 32

Mini focaccia with roasted vegetables

2 red capsicums (pepper)
2 yellow capsicums (pepper)
3 slender eggplants (aubergine)
2 large zucchini (courgette)
1 red onion
1/3 cup (80 ml) extra virgin olive oil
3 cloves garlic, crushed
12 mini focaccias, halved
1/4 cup (60 g) ready-made pesto
3 large bocconcini, sliced

Preheat the oven to moderately hot 200°C (400°F/Gas 6). Cut the red and yellow capsicums into 3 cm pieces. Slice the eggplants and zucchini into 1 cm rounds, then thinly slice the onion. Place all the vegetables in a roasting tin with the oil and garlic, then season with salt and cracked black pepper and toss together thoroughly. Roast for 25 minutes, or until cooked.

Spread each half of the focaccia with 1/2 teaspoon of the pesto and divide the vegetables among them. Place two slices of bocconcini on top of each base, then top with the lid. Toast the focaccias on both sides on a hot chargrill pan until heated through.

Slice each focaccia in half, then wrap a 3 cm wide band of double greaseproof paper around the middle of the sandwiches and secure with string. Serve warm.

Makes 24

Ratatouille pies

¼ cup (60 ml) olive oil
1 eggplant (aubergine), diced
1 onion, finely chopped
1 red capsicum (pepper), diced
1 small zucchini (courgette), diced
1 tablespoon tomato paste (purée)
200 g tomatoes, chopped
1 teaspoon dried Italian herbs
750 g ready-made shortcrust pastry
1 egg, lightly beaten
ready-made pesto, to serve

Heat 2 tablespoons of the oil in a frying pan and cook the eggplant until golden. Remove from the pan. Heat the remaining oil in the pan, add the onion, capsicum and zucchini and cook for 2 minutes. Stir in the tomato paste, fresh tomato, herbs and eggplant. Cook for 20 minutes, or until reduced. Allow to cool.

Meanwhile, preheat the oven to moderate 180°C (350°F/Gas 4) and put a baking tray in the oven. Grease 24 mini muffin holes. Roll the pastry thinly and cut out 24 rounds with a 7 cm cutter. Repeat with a 5.5 cm cutter. Put one of the larger rounds in each muffin hole and fill with the cooled filling. Dampen the edges of the small rounds and place them on top of the filling to seal the pies. Brush with egg. Put the tin on the hot baking tray and cook for 25 minutes, or until golden. Cool slightly, then remove from the tin. Serve with pesto.

Makes 24

Mini crab cakes with coriander paste

1 tablespoon butter
4 spring onions, thinly sliced
1 egg
2 tablespoons sour cream
350 g fresh white crab meat, excess
   liquid squeezed out
1 small yellow capsicum (pepper),
   finely diced
2 teaspoons chopped fresh thyme
2½ cups (200 g) fresh white
   breadcrumbs
olive oil, for shallow-frying

Coriander paste
1 clove garlic
1 green chilli, seeded
½ teaspoon ground cumin
¼ teaspoon sugar
¾ cup (25 g) fresh coriander leaves
½ cup (10 g) fresh mint
1 tablespoon lemon juice
25 ml coconut cream
½ avocado

Line a tray with baking paper. Melt the butter in a frying pan over low heat. When it begins to foam, add the spring onion and cook for 2 minutes, or until softened. Remove from the heat and cool.

Mix the egg and sour cream until just smooth. Add the spring onion, crab, capsicum, thyme and ½ cup (40 g) of the breadcrumbs, season and mix together. Shape the mixture into flat rounds, using 1 level tablespoon for each. Place on the tray and refrigerate for 30 minutes.

Meanwhile, to make the coriander paste, process the garlic, chilli, cumin, sugar, herbs, lemon juice and ¼ teaspoon salt in a food processor until a fine paste forms. Add the coconut cream and continue to blend until smooth. Add the avocado and, using the pulse action, process until just smooth. Transfer to a bowl, cover with plastic wrap and chill.

Using your hands, coat the crab cakes in the remaining breadcrumbs. Heat enough olive oil in a non-stick frying pan to just coat the bottom. Cook in batches for 2–3 minutes each side, or until golden. Drain and serve warm with ½ teaspoon of coriander paste on each.

Makes 24

Thai chicken balls

1 kg chicken mince
1 cup (80 g) fresh breadcrumbs
4 spring onions, sliced
1 tablespoon ground coriander
1 cup (50 g) chopped fresh coriander
3 tablespoons sweet chilli sauce
1–2 tablespoons lemon juice
oil, for frying

Preheat the oven to moderately hot 200°C (400°F/Gas 6). Mix the mince and breadcrumbs in a large bowl.

Add the spring onion, ground and fresh coriander, chilli sauce and lemon juice and mix well. Using damp hands, form the mixture into evenly shaped balls that are either small enough to eat with your fingers or large enough to use as burgers.

Heat the oil in a deep frying pan, and shallow-fry the chicken balls in batches over high heat until browned all over. Place them on a baking tray and bake until cooked through. (Small chicken balls will take 5 minutes to cook and larger ones will take 10–15 minutes.) The mixture makes a delicious filling for sausage rolls.

Serves 6

Lamb korma on mini poppadoms

350 g lamb backstrap or fillet, cut into 1.5 cm cubes
2 tablespoons korma curry paste
1 clove garlic, crushed
1 teaspoon ground coriander
1/2 cup (125 g) thick plain yoghurt
oil, for deep-frying
24 round 4 cm poppadoms (chilli flavour, if available)
1 tablespoon oil, extra
1 1/2 tablespoons mango chutney
small fresh coriander leaves, to garnish

Combine the lamb, curry paste, garlic, ground coriander and half the yoghurt in a non-metallic bowl. Cover and refrigerate for 1–2 hours.

Meanwhile, fill a deep heavy-based saucepan or deep-fryer one-third full of oil and heat to 180°C (350°F), or until a cube of bread browns in 15 seconds. Cook the poppadoms a few at a time for a few seconds each, or until they are puffed and lightly golden. Remove with a slotted spoon and drain on crumpled paper towels.

Heat a wok over high heat, add the extra oil and swirl to coat. Add the marinated lamb and cook in batches, stirring, for 4–5 minutes, or until the lamb is cooked through. Spoon a heaped teaspoon onto each poppadom and top with 1/2 teaspoon of the remaining yoghurt, then 1/4 teaspoon of the chutney. Garnish with a coriander leaf and serve immediately.

Makes 24

Think ahead: Lamb korma can be cooked and frozen for up to 2 months, or refrigerated for 2–3 days. Reheat in a saucepan over low heat until warm. Variations: You can make chicken korma instead, by replacing the lamb with 350 g diced chicken tenderloins.

Mini hamburgers

8 burger buns, split in half
400 g beef mince
¼ cup (25 g) dry breadcrumbs
3 French shallots, very finely chopped
1 tablespoon Dijon mustard
1 tablespoon Worcestershire sauce
⅓ cup (80 ml) tomato sauce
olive oil, for shallow-frying
100 g thinly sliced Cheddar, cut into
   24 squares, each 3 cm
24 baby rocket leaves, stems
   removed and torn into 2.5 cm
   pieces
12 cornichons (baby gherkins), cut
   into thin slices

Stamp out rounds from the burger buns using a 4 cm cutter; you should get 24 from the tops and 24 from the bases. If the buns are quite thick, trim them with a serrated knife after you have cut them.

Combine the mince, breadcrumbs, chopped French shallots, mustard, Worcestershire sauce, 1 tablespoon of the tomato sauce and some salt and cracked black pepper in a bowl. Divide the mixture into 24 walnut-sized pieces. With wet hands, shape the pieces into patties.

Heat a large heavy-based frying pan with enough oil to just cover the bottom of the pan and cook the patties over medium heat for about 1 minute on each side, or until browned, then place on a baking tray.

Lightly grill both halves of the mini burger buns. Top each patty with a small slice of cheese and grill for 1 minute, or until the cheese is just starting to melt.

Place the patties on the bottom halves of the burger buns. Top with the rocket, cornichon and remaining tomato sauce. Gently press on the top half of the burger bun and secure with a cocktail stick. Serve warm.

Makes 24

Vegetable samosas

2 tablespoons ghee or oil
1 small onion, diced
1 tablespoon hot curry paste
200 g potatoes, cut into 1 cm cubes
150 g orange sweet potato, peeled
  and cut into 1 cm cubes
1 tablespoon soft brown sugar
½ cup (80 g) frozen peas
⅓ cup (50 g) salted roasted cashew
  nuts, chopped
½ cup (25 g) roughly chopped fresh
  coriander leaves
1 kg (5 sheets) shortcrust pastry
oil, for deep-frying

Dipping sauce
2 cups (500 g) thick Greek-style
  yoghurt
1 cup (30 g) fresh coriander leaves,
  roughly chopped
1 teaspoon ground cumin

Heat the ghee in a large heavy-based saucepan over medium heat. Cook the onion and hot curry paste for 5 minutes, stirring regularly until fragrant and the onion is golden. Add the potato, orange sweet potato and sugar. Cook, stirring regularly, for 8–10 minutes, or until the potatoes are tender. Stir in the peas, reduce the heat to low, cover and cook for a further 5 minutes. If the mixture is sticking, add 1–2 tablespoons of water. Cool to room temperature.

To make the dipping sauce, combine all the ingredients in a bowl and chill until needed.

Season the vegetable mixture then add the cashews and coriander. Using a 7 cm cutter, cut nine circles from each sheet of pastry. Place 1 rounded teaspoon of filling in the middle of each circle. Fold the pastry over and pinch the sides together.

Fill a deep heavy-based saucepan one-third full of oil and heat to 170°C (325°F), or until a cube of bread browns in 20 seconds. Deep-fry 4 samosas at a time for 3 minutes, or until crisp and the pastry has 'blistered' a little. Drain on paper towels. Serve warm with the dipping sauce.

Makes 45

Mini eggs Florentine

Hollandaise sauce
3 egg yolks
2 tablespoons lime or lemon juice
125 g butter, melted

6–8 slices bread
oil spray
24 quail eggs
250 g English spinach, trimmed

Preheat the oven to moderate 180°C (350°F/Gas 4). To make the hollandaise sauce, blend the yolks and juice in a food processor for 5 seconds, then gradually add the melted butter. Transfer to a bowl and refrigerate for about 30 minutes, until thickened.

Cut 24 rounds of bread with a 4 cm cutter. Place on a baking tray, spray with oil and bake for 10 minutes. Turn over and bake for another 5 minutes, until dry and crisp.

Put about 2.5 cm water in a large non-stick frying pan and bring to simmering point. Reduce the heat so the water is not moving. Carefully crack the eggs into the water. Spoon a little water onto the top of the eggs as they cook, and when set, remove and drain on paper towels.

Steam or microwave the spinach for 2 minutes, or until wilted, then drain well. To assemble, put some spinach on the bread rounds, then top with egg and drizzle with hollandaise. Serve immediately.

Makes 24

Note: Quail eggs are available from speciality food stores or can be ordered from poultry shops. You can use bottled hollandaise.

Turkish pizza

Basic pizza dough
10 g dried yeast
1 teaspoon caster sugar
4 cups (500 g) plain flour
2 tablespoons olive oil

1 tablespoon olive oil, plus extra
  for brushing
375 g lamb mince
1 onion, finely chopped
1/4 cup (40 g) pine nuts
1 tomato, peeled, seeded and
  chopped
1/4 teaspoon ground cinnamon
pinch of allspice
2 teaspoons chopped fresh coriander,
  plus extra for serving
2 teaspoons lemon juice
1/4 cup (60 g) plain yoghurt

Combine the yeast, sugar and 3/4 cup
(185 ml) warm water. Cover and leave
for 10 minutes, or until frothy. If it
hasn't foamed after 10 minutes,
discard and start again.

Sift the flour and 1/2 teaspoon salt and
make a well. Add the yeast mixture
and oil. Mix with a flat-bladed knife,
using a cutting action, until a dough
forms. Knead for 10 minutes, or until
smooth. Place in an oiled bowl, cover
with plastic wrap and leave for
45 minutes, or until doubled in size.

Heat the oil in a frying pan over
medium heat and cook the mince
for 3 minutes, or until browned. Add
the onion and cook over low heat for
8 minutes, or until soft. Add the pine
nuts, tomato, spices, 1/4 teaspoon
cracked pepper and some salt. Cook
for 8 minutes, or until dry. Stir in the
coriander and lemon juice and season.

Preheat the oven to very hot 230°C
(450°F/Gas 8). Punch down the
dough, then knead for 8 minutes,
or until elastic. Roll out into 24 ovals.
Spoon some filling onto each base.
Pinch together the two short sides to
form a boat shape. Brush with oil, and
place the pizzas on a greased baking
tray. Bake for 10 minutes. Serve with
a dab of yoghurt and some coriander.

Makes 24

Olive and potato balls with pesto

650 g floury potatoes (e.g. russet, King Edward)
1 tablespoon olive oil
1 onion, finely chopped
2 cloves garlic, finely chopped
$\frac{1}{2}$ cup (80 g) pitted Kalamata olives, sliced
$\frac{1}{3}$ cup (40 g) plain flour
$\frac{1}{4}$ cup (25 g) grated Parmesan
$\frac{1}{4}$ cup (15 g) shredded fresh basil
1 egg
$\frac{3}{4}$ cup (45 g) dry Japanese breadcrumbs
oil, for deep-frying
$\frac{1}{4}$ cup (60 g) ready-made pesto
2 slices prosciutto, sliced into thin strips

Cut the potatoes into 4 cm chunks and steam or boil for 15 minutes, or until tender. Drain well, then mash.

Heat the olive oil in a frying pan and cook the onion over medium heat for 4–5 minutes, or until soft. Add the garlic and cook for an extra minute. Remove from the heat, cool and add to the potato. Mix in the olives, flour, Parmesan, basil and egg, and a little salt and cracked black pepper. Shape the mixture into 30 small balls, then refrigerate for 30 minutes. Roll the balls in breadcrumbs, pressing the breadcrumbs on firmly so that the balls are evenly coated.

Fill a deep heavy-based saucepan or deep-fryer one-third full of oil and heat to 180°C (350°F), or until a cube of bread browns in 15 seconds. Cook the olive and potato balls in batches for 2–3 minutes, or until golden. Drain on crumpled paper towels. Top each one with $\frac{1}{2}$ teaspoon of the pesto and a piece of prosciutto.

Makes 30

Note: The Japanese breadcrumbs provide a good crisp coating, but you can also use normal breadcrumbs. Think ahead: The balls can be frozen for up to 2 months before cooking or refrigerated for 2 days.

Lemon grass prawns

6 lemon grass stalks, cut in half
   lengthways, then in half crossways
1 kg peeled and deveined prawns
3 spring onions, roughly chopped
4 tablespoons fresh coriander leaves
2 tablespoons fresh mint
2 tablespoons fish sauce
1½ tablespoons lime juice
1–2 tablespoons sweet chilli sauce,
   plus extra for serving
peanut oil, for brushing

Soak the lemon grass in water for 30 minutes, then pat dry. Process the prawns, spring onion, coriander, mint, fish sauce, lime juice and chilli sauce in a food processor. Take a tablespoon of the mix and mould around the end of a lemon grass stalk, using wet hands. Refrigerate for 30 minutes.

Brush a barbecue hotplate or chargrill pan with the oil. Cook the skewers, turning occasionally, for 5 minutes, or until cooked. Serve with sweet chilli sauce.

Makes 24

Empanadas

2 eggs
40 g (1 1/4 oz) stuffed green olives,
  chopped
95 g (3 oz) ham, finely chopped
1/4 cup (30 g/1 oz) grated Cheddar
3 sheets ready-rolled puff pastry,
  thawed
1 egg yolk, lightly beaten

Place the eggs in a small saucepan,
cover with water and bring to the boil.
Boil for 10 minutes, then drain and
cool for 5 minutes in cold water. Peel
and chop.

Preheat the oven to hot 220°C (425°F/
Gas 7). Lightly grease two baking
trays. Combine the egg, olives, ham
and Cheddar in a large bowl.

Cut five 10 cm rounds from each
pastry sheet. Place a tablespoon
of the filling into the centre of each
round, fold the pastry over and crimp
the edges to seal.

Place the pastries on the trays, about
2 cm apart. Brush with the egg yolk
and bake in the centre or top half of
the oven for 15 minutes, or until well
browned and puffed. Swap the trays
around after 10 minutes and cover
loosely with foil if the empanadas
start to brown too much. Serve hot.

Makes 15

Moroccan lamb pies

Filling

2 tablespoons olive oil
1 onion, thinly sliced
2 cloves garlic, crushed
2 teaspoons ground cumin
2 teaspoons ground ginger
2 teaspoons paprika
1 teaspoon ground turmeric
1 teaspoon ground cinnamon
500 g lamb fillet, diced
1½ cups (375 ml) beef stock
1 tablespoon finely chopped
  preserved lemon
2 tablespoons sliced Kalamata olives
1 tablespoon chopped fresh coriander
24 pastry shells

750 g shortcrust pastry
1 egg, lightly beaten

Heat the oil in a large saucepan over medium heat, then add the onion, garlic and spices. Add the lamb to the pan and coat in the spice mixture. Pour in the stock, cover and cook over low heat for 30 minutes. Add the lemon and cook, uncovered, for a further 20 minutes, or until the liquid has reduced and the lamb is tender. Stir in the olives and coriander and allow to cool.

Meanwhile, heat the oven to moderate 180°C (350°F/Gas 4) and put a baking tray in the oven. Grease 24 mini muffin holes. Roll the pastry thinly and cut out 24 rounds with a 7 cm cutter. Repeat with a 5.5 cm cutter. Put one of the larger rounds in each muffin hole and fill with the cooled filling. Dampen the edges of the small rounds and place them on top of the filling to seal the pies. Brush with the egg. Put the tin on the hot baking tray and cook for 25 minutes, or until golden. Cool slightly, then remove from the tin. Delicious served with a dollop of plain yoghurt.

Makes 24

Peking duck rolls

1 cup (125 g) plain flour
1/2 teaspoon sesame oil
1/2 large Chinese roast duck
6 spring onions, cut into 6 cm lengths
  (24 pieces in total)
1 Lebanese cucumber, seeded and
  cut into 6 cm x 5 mm batons
2–3 tablespoons hoisin sauce
2 teaspoons toasted sesame seeds
24 chives, blanched

Sift the flour, make a well in the centre, and pour in the sesame oil and 1/2 cup (125 ml) boiling water. Stir until the mixture forms a slightly sticky, soft dough. Add a few teaspoons of boiling water if required. Knead on a floured surface for about 5 minutes, or until smooth. Cover and rest for about 10 minutes.

Shred the duck into pieces and cut the skin into small strips.

Divide the dough into 24 pieces, then roll each piece to an 8–9 cm round on a floured board. Cover with plastic wrap while you are working, to prevent them from drying out.

Heat a non-stick frying pan over medium–high heat and dry fry the pancakes for about 20 seconds each side. Do not overcook, or they will become too crispy for rolling. Stack on a plate and keep warm. If required, reheat by wrapping in foil and baking in a warm (170°C/325°F/Gas 3) oven until warmed through, or microwave for 20–30 seconds on high.

Arrange a piece of spring onion, cucumber, duck flesh and skin on each pancake. Add 1/2 teaspoon hoisin and sprinkle with sesame seeds. Roll firmly and tie each with a chive.

Makes 24

Goat's cheese fritters with roasted capsicum sauce

Roasted capsicum sauce
2 red capsicums (pepper)
2 tablespoons olive oil
1 small red onion, finely chopped
1 clove garlic
1/3 cup (80 ml) chicken or vegetable
  stock

420 g ricotta cheese, well drained
400 g goat's cheese, crumbled
2 tablespoons chopped fresh chives
1/4 cup (30 g) flour
2 eggs, lightly beaten
1 cup (100 g) dry breadcrumbs
oil, for deep-frying

Cut the capsicums into 2–3 pieces, removing the seeds and membrane. Place, skin-side-up, under a hot grill until the skin blackens and blisters. Cool in a plastic bag, then peel away the skin and roughly chop the flesh.

Heat the olive oil in a frying pan over medium heat and cook the onion and garlic for 5 minutes, or until softened. Add the capsicum and stock. Bring to the boil, then remove from the heat, cool slightly and transfer to a food processor. Pulse until combined, but still a little lumpy. Season and refrigerate until needed.

Combine the ricotta, goat's cheese and chives in a bowl. Add the flour and eggs, then season and mix well.

Put the breadcrumbs in a bowl. Roll a tablespoon of the cheese mixture into a ball with damp hands, flatten slightly and coat in the breadcrumbs. Repeat with the remaining mixture. Refrigerate for 30 minutes.

Fill a deep heavy-based saucepan one-third full of oil and heat to 180°C (350°F), or until a cube of bread browns in 15 seconds. Cook the fritters in batches for 1 minute, or until browned, then drain. Serve warm with the capsicum sauce.

Makes 30

Tofu and vegetable koftas with yoghurt dipping sauce

Yoghurt dipping sauce
200 g plain soy yoghurt
1 clove garlic, crushed
2 tablespoons fresh mint, finely
  chopped

250 g firm tofu
4 tablespoons olive oil
1½ cups (185 g) grated pumpkin
  (see Note)
¾ cup (100 g) grated zucchini
  (courgette) (see Note)
1 onion, chopped
4 cloves garlic, crushed
4 small spring onions, finely chopped
¼ cup (7 g) chopped fresh coriander
  leaves
1 tablespoon Madras curry powder
1 cup (150 g) wholemeal flour
½ cup (50 g) grated Parmesan
oil, for deep-frying

To make the dipping sauce, place the yoghurt, garlic and mint in a bowl, season and mix together well. Add a little water, if needed.

Blend the tofu in a food processor or blender until finely processed.

Heat the oil in a frying pan. Add the pumpkin, zucchini, onion and garlic and cook over medium heat, stirring occasionally, for 10 minutes, or until the vegetables are tender. Cool.

Add the spring onion, coriander, curry powder, ½ cup (75 g) of the wholemeal flour, Parmesan, tofu and 1 tablespoon salt and mix well. Roll a tablespoon of the mixture between your hands to form a ball, then repeat with the remaining mixture. Coat the balls in the remaining flour.

Fill a deep heavy-based saucepan one-third full of oil and heat to 180°C (350°F), or until a cube of bread browns in 15 seconds. Cook the tofu and vegetable koftas in small batches for 2–3 minutes, or until golden brown. Drain on paper towels. Serve with the dipping sauce.

Serves 4

Note: When buying the vegetables, buy a piece of pumpkin that weighs about 400 g and 200 g zucchini.

Grilled prawns with tequila mayonnaise

24 raw king prawns
1/3 cup (80 ml) olive oil
2 tablespoons lime juice
1 tablespoon tequila
2/3 cup (160 g) whole-egg
   mayonnaise

Peel and devein the prawns, keeping the tails intact. Combine the olive oil with the lime juice in a non-metallic bowl and season with salt and cracked black pepper. Add the prawns, cover and leave to marinate for 1 hour. Meanwhile, mix the tequila into the mayonnaise, then transfer to a serving dish.

Heat a barbecue or chargrill pan to hot, add the prawns and cook for 1–2 minutes on each side until pink and cooked through. Serve with the tequila mayonnaise for dipping.

Makes 24

Think ahead: The prawns can be grilled up to an hour beforehand. One way to save time is to buy pre-cooked prawns from your fishmonger. Then all you need to do is to peel them, leaving the tails intact. Squeeze them with lime juice and serve with the mayonnaise.
Variation: If you prefer to have a dipping sauce without alcohol, simply add 2 tablespoons of chopped fresh herbs, such as dill, basil or parsley to the mayonnaise instead of the tequila. Alternatively, add a teaspoon of grated lemon or lime zest for a fresh citrus flavour.

Petit Croque-Monsieur

1 loaf of bread, sliced into 6 slices
    lengthways
½ cup (125 g) wholegrain mustard
100 g thinly shaved honey ham
100 g thinly sliced Jarlsberg cheese
⅓ cup (55 g) very finely chopped
    mustard fruits (optional) (see Note)
40 g butter
2 tablespoons olive oil

Brush each slice of bread with
1 tablespoon of mustard. Divide the
ham and cheese into three portions
and lay one portion of the ham, then
the cheese, on three bread slices. If
you are using mustard fruits, sprinkle
them over the cheese. Press the other
bread slices, mustard-side-down, on
top so that you have three large
sandwiches. Cut eight rounds from
each sandwich with a 5 cm cutter.
Melt half the butter and oil in a non-
stick frying pan and, when the butter
begins to foam, cook half the rounds
until crisp and golden and the cheese
is just starting to melt. Keep warm on
a baking tray in a warm oven while
you cook the remaining rounds.
Serve warm.

Makes 24

Note: Mustard fruits are also known
as mostarda di frutta.
Variation: To transform the Croque-
Monsieur to a Croque-Madame, fry
24 quail eggs in a little oil and butter.
Then, stamp a neat circle out of the
egg with a 5 cm cutter. Place an egg
on top of each sandwich.

Mini spinach pies

⅓ cup (80 ml) olive oil
2 onions, finely chopped
2 cloves garlic, chopped
150 g small button mushrooms,
  roughly chopped
200 g English spinach, chopped
½ teaspoon chopped fresh thyme
100 g feta cheese, crumbled
750 g bought shortcrust pastry
milk, to glaze

Heat 2 tablespoons of the oil in a frying pan over medium heat, add the onion and garlic and cook for 5 minutes, or until soft and lightly coloured. Add the mushrooms and cook for another 4 minutes, or until softened. Transfer to a bowl.

Heat 1 tablespoon of the oil in the same pan over medium heat, add half the spinach and cook, stirring well, for 2–3 minutes, or until the spinach has softened. Add to the bowl with the onion. Repeat with the remaining oil and spinach. Add the thyme and feta to the bowl and mix. Season with salt and pepper and set aside to cool.

Preheat the oven to moderately hot 200°C (400°F/Gas 6) and grease two 12-hole round-based patty tins. Roll out half the pastry between two sheets of baking paper and cut out 24 rounds using a 7.5 cm cutter. Use these to line the patty tins, then divide the spinach mixture among the holes. Roll out the remaining pastry between the baking paper and cut into 24 x 7 cm rounds to fit the tops of the pies. Cover the pies with the lids and press the edges with a fork to seal. Prick the tops once with a fork, brush with milk and bake for 15–20 minutes, or until golden. Serve immediately or cool on a wire rack.

Makes 24

Feta, rocket and mushroom bruschetta

1 loaf Italian bread
1 large clove garlic, peeled
extra virgin olive oil, to drizzle
1 tablespoon olive oil
60 g butter
300 g small Swiss brown mushrooms,
  cut into quarters
2 cloves garlic, crushed
¼ cup (7 g) roughly torn fresh basil
150 g soft marinated feta cheese
50 g baby rocket leaves

Preheat the oven to moderately hot 200°C (400°F/Gas 6). Slice the loaf of bread on the diagonal into twelve 1 cm thick slices. Lay the bread slices out in a single layer on a baking tray and bake for 10–12 minutes, or until they are lightly golden. Remove from the oven and rub the garlic clove over one side of each slice of toast. Lightly drizzle each slice with extra virgin olive oil, then cut them in half again so that each piece is easily handled by your guests.

Heat the oil and butter in a frying pan over high heat until the butter has melted, then add the mushrooms and cook for 3–4 minutes. Add the garlic and cook for a further minute. Remove the pan from the heat and stir in the basil, then season with some salt and cracked black pepper. Spread the feta on the prepared bruschetta, then add a few rocket leaves. To finish, top with some of the fried mushrooms, and serve immediately.

Makes 24

Note: Bruschetta are best made at the last moment to prevent the bread drying out or the toppings from making the bread soggy.

Sweet

Mixed nut tartlets

300 g mixed nuts (pecans,
   macadamia nuts or hazelnuts)
3 cups (375 g) plain flour
230 g butter, chopped
3 tablespoons soft brown sugar
2 tablespoons white sugar
3 tablespoons light corn syrup
30 g butter, melted
2 eggs, lightly beaten

Preheat the oven to moderate 180°C
(350°F/Gas 4). Spread the nuts on a
baking tray and bake for 7 minutes.

Place the sifted flour and butter in a
food processor. Pulse for 10 seconds,
or until the mixture resembles fine
breadcrumbs. Add about 1/3 cup
(80 ml) water and process until the
mixture just comes together. Add
another tablespoon of water if
needed. Turn out onto a lightly
floured surface and gather into
a ball. Refrigerate for 20 minutes.

Divide the pastry into 10 portions. Roll
each portion out on a lightly floured
surface and line 10 fluted, 8 cm flan
tins. Trim any excess pastry, then
refrigerate for 10 minutes. Put the
tins on two baking trays. Cut sheets
of crumpled baking paper to line the
base and side of each tin. Place
baking beads or rice in the tins and
bake for 10 minutes. Remove the
beads and paper and bake for
10–15 minutes.

Divide the nuts among the pastry
shells. Whisk together the remaining
ingredients and drizzle the mixture
over the nuts. Bake for 15–20 minutes,
or until just set and golden. Allow to
cool completely before serving.

Makes 10

Watermelon and vodka granita

1 kg piece of watermelon, rind
  removed to give 600 g flesh
2 teaspoons lime juice
¼ cup (60 g) caster sugar
¼ cup (60 ml) citrus-flavoured vodka

Coarsely chop the watermelon, removing the seeds. Place the flesh in a food processor and add the lime juice and sugar. Process until smooth, then strain through a fine sieve. Stir in the vodka, then taste — if the watermelon is not very sweet, you may have to add a little more sugar.

Pour into a shallow 1.5 litre metal tin and freeze for about 1 hour, or until beginning to freeze around the edges. Scrape the frozen parts back into the mixture with a fork. Repeat every 30 minutes for about 4 hours, or until even ice crystals have formed.

Serve immediately or beat with a fork just before serving. To serve, scrape into dishes with a fork.

Serves 4–6

Serving suggestion: A scoop of the granita in a shot glass with vodka is a hit at summer cocktail parties.
Variation: A tablespoon of finely chopped mint may be stirred through the mixture after straining the liquid.

Hazelnut biscotti with Frangelico shots

1³/₄ cups (215 g) plain flour
²/₃ cup (160 g) caster sugar
¹/₂ teaspoon baking powder
60 g chilled unsalted butter, cubed
2 eggs
1¹/₄ cups (150 g) roughly chopped
  roasted hazelnuts
2 teaspoons grated orange zest
¹/₂ teaspoon caster sugar, extra

Frangelico shot
¹/₄ cup (60 ml) double-strength coffee
  per person
1–2 teaspoons Frangelico per person

Preheat the oven to moderate 180°C (350°F/Gas 4) and line two baking trays with baking paper. Place the sifted flour, sugar, baking powder and a pinch of salt in a food processor and mix for 2 seconds. Add the butter and pulse until the mixture resembles breadcrumbs. Add the eggs and process until it comes together.

Transfer the dough to a floured surface and knead in the hazelnuts and zest. Divide into two portions and, using floured hands, shape each into a log about 20 cm long. Place on the baking trays and sprinkle with the extra sugar. Press the top of each log down gently to flatten slightly. Bake for 20 minutes, or until golden. Remove and cool for 20 minutes. Reduce the oven temperature to warm 160°C (315°F/Gas 2–3).

Cut the logs into 5 mm–1 cm slices on the diagonal (at least 6 cm long). Turn the baking paper over, then spread on the tray in a single layer. Return to the oven and bake for a further 20–25 minutes, or until just begining to colour. Cool completely before storing in an airtight container.

To make the Frangelico shot, pour hot coffee into shot glasses and top with Frangelico to taste.

Makes 40

Nougat

2 cups (500 g) sugar
1 cup (250 ml) liquid glucose
½ cup (175 g) honey (preferably
  blossom honey)
2 egg whites
1 teaspoon vanilla essence
125 g unsalted butter, softened
60 g almonds, unblanched and
  toasted
100 g glacé cherries

Grease a 28 x 18 cm baking dish and line with baking paper. Stir the sugar, glucose, honey, ¼ cup (60 ml) water and ¼ teaspoon salt over low heat in a heavy-based saucepan until dissolved. Bring to the boil and cook at a rolling boil for 8 minutes, or until the mixture forms a hard ball when tested in water or reaches 122°C (225°F) on a sugar thermometer. The correct temperature is very important, otherwise it will not set properly.

Beat the egg whites with electric beaters until stiff peaks form. Slowly add a quarter of the sugar mixture to the egg whites and beat for 5 minutes, or until it holds its shape. Cook the remaining syrup for 2 minutes, or until a small amount forms brittle threads when dropped in cold water, or reaches 157°C (315°F) on a sugar thermometer. Add slowly to the meringue mixture with the beaters running, and beat until very thick.

Add the vanilla and butter, and beat for another 5 minutes. Stir in the almonds and cherries with a metal spoon. Turn the mixture into the tin and smooth the top. Chill for at least four hours, or until firm. Turn onto a large board and cut into 4 x 2 cm pieces. Wrap each piece in cellophane and store in the refrigerator.

Makes 1 kg

Mini cherry galettes

670 g jar pitted morello cherries,
  drained
30 g unsalted butter
1½ tablespoons caster sugar
1 egg yolk
½ teaspoon vanilla essence
½ cup (95 g) ground almonds
1 tablespoon plain flour
2 sheets ready-rolled puff pastry,
  thawed
icing sugar, for dusting
½ cup (160 g) cherry jam

Preheat the oven to moderate 180°C (350°F/Gas 4). Line a baking tray with baking paper. Spread the cherries on several sheets of paper towel to absorb any excess liquid. Combine the butter and sugar and beat until creamy. Add the egg yolk and vanilla, then stir in the combined almonds and flour and chill until required.

Cut 30 rounds from the pastry sheets using a 5 cm round cutter. Place half the rounds on the prepared tray and lightly prick them all over with a fork. Cover with another sheet of baking paper and weigh down with another baking tray—this prevents the pastry from rising during cooking. Cook for 10 minutes, remove from the oven and allow to cool on the trays. Repeat with the remaining rounds. Leave the oven on.

Place 1 level teaspoon of almond mixture in the centre of each cooled pastry round, then press three cherries onto the almond mixture.

Bake for another 10 minutes or until lightly browned. Cool slightly then dust lightly with icing sugar. Place the jam in a cup, stand in a saucepan of hot water and stir until melted. Glaze the cherries by brushing them with the warmed jam.

Makes 30

Hazelnut cream squares

4 eggs, separated
½ cup (125 g) caster sugar
½ cup (60 g) self-raising flour
⅔ cup (75 g) ground hazelnuts
150 g unsalted butter, softened
½ cup (170 g) chocolate hazelnut
  spread
½ cup (60 g) icing sugar, sifted
cocoa powder, to dust

Preheat the oven to moderate 180°C (350°F/Gas 4). Grease a 20 cm shallow square cake tin and line the base with baking paper. Beat the egg whites with electric beaters in a bowl until soft peaks form. Gradually add the sugar, beating until thick and glossy. Beat the egg yolks into the mixture, one at a time.

Sift the flour over the mixture, add the ground hazelnuts and fold in with a metal spoon. Melt 20 g of the butter with 2 tablespoons boiling water in a small bowl, then fold into the sponge mixture. Pour the mixture into the prepared tin and bake for 25 minutes, or until cooked. Leave in the tin for 5 minutes before turning out onto a wire rack to cool. Cut the sponge in half horizontally through the centre.

Beat the hazelnut spread and the remaining butter with electric beaters until very creamy. Beat in the icing sugar, then gradually add 3 teaspoons of boiling water and beat until smooth. Fill the cake with the icing mixture and refrigerate until the filling is firm. Dust with the cocoa powder then cut into squares.

Makes 16

Choc-dipped
ice cream balls

500 g good-quality ice cream (use
    vanilla or a mixture of vanilla,
    pistachio and chocolate)
150 g dark chocolate
150 g white chocolate
150 g milk chocolate
2 tablespoons toasted shelled
    walnuts, roughly chopped
2 tablespoons shelled pistachios,
    roughly chopped
2 tablespoons toasted shredded
    coconut

Line two large baking trays with
baking paper and place in the freezer
to chill. Working quickly, use a melon
baller to form 36 balls of ice cream
and place on the chilled baking trays.
Place a cocktail stick in each ice
cream ball. Return to the freezer
for 1 hour to freeze hard.

Place the chocolate in three separate
heatproof bowls. Bring a saucepan of
water to the boil, then remove the pan
from the heat. Sit one bowl at a time
over the pan, making sure the base
of the bowl does not sit in the water.
Stir occasionally until the chocolate
has melted. Remove the bowl from
the heat and set aside to cool; the
chocolate should remain liquid; if it
hardens, repeat.

Put the walnuts, pistachios and
coconut in three separate small
bowls. Working with 12 of the ice
cream balls, dip one at a time quickly
in the dark chocolate, then into the
bowl with the walnuts. Return to
the freezer. Repeat the process
with another 12 balls, dipping them
in the melted white chocolate and
the pistachios. Dip the last 12 balls
in the milk chocolate, then the toasted
coconut. Freeze all the ice cream balls
for 1 hour.

Makes 36

Grape fritters with cinnamon sugar

Cinnamon sugar
2 tablespoons caster sugar
1 teaspoon ground cinnamon

2 eggs, separated
1/2 teaspoon vanilla essence
1/4 cup (60 g) caster sugar
150 g seedless red or black grapes
1/3 cup (40 g) self-raising flour
40 g unsalted butter

To make the cinnamon sugar, combine the sugar and cinnamon in a bowl.

Whisk the egg yolks with the vanilla and sugar until combined and just creamy. Slice each grape into four slices, then stir the grape slices into the egg yolk mixture. Sift the flour into the egg mixture. Beat the egg whites in a clean bowl until soft peaks form. Lightly fold half of the egg whites into the egg yolk mixture with a metal spoon until just combined, then repeat with the rest of the egg whites.

Melt 2 teaspoons of the butter in a frying pan over low heat. Place 6 heaped teaspoons of the batter into the pan to make six fritters. Cook over low–medium heat for 2–3 minutes, turning very carefully when the base becomes firm and bubbles appear around the edges. Cook for a further 1–2 minutes, or until golden. Remove to a plate and keep warm. Repeat to make 24 fritters. Dust the fritters with cinnamon sugar and serve warm.

Makes 24

Think ahead: The fritters are best made as close to serving as possible on the day they are to be served. If necessary, they can be heated in a warm (170°C/325°F/Gas 3) oven for 5 minutes. Sprinkle them with sugar just before serving.

Portuguese custard tarts

1¼ cups (155 g) plain flour
25 g vegetable shortening, chopped
    and softened
30 g butter, chopped and softened
1 cup (250 g) sugar
2 cups (500 ml) milk
3 tablespoons cornflour
1 tablespoon custard powder
4 egg yolks
1 teaspoon vanilla essence

Sift the flour and add about ¾ cup
(185 ml) water, or enough to form a
soft dough. Gather into a ball, then
roll out on non-stick baking paper to
form a 24 x 30 cm rectangle. Spread
with the vegetable shortening and roll
up from the short edge.

Roll the dough out into a rectangle
again, and spread with the butter.
Roll up again into a log and slice
into 12 even pieces. Working from the
centre outwards, use your fingertips
to press each piece out to a circle
that is large enough to cover the base
and sides of twelve ⅓-cup (80 ml)
muffin holes. Press into the tin and
refrigerate while preparing the filling.

Stir the sugar and ⅓ cup (80 ml) of
water over low heat until the sugar
dissolves. Mix a little milk with the
cornflour and custard powder to
form a smooth paste. Add to the
pan with the remaining milk, egg
yolks and vanilla. Stir over low heat
until the mixture thickens. Put in a
bowl, cover and cool.

Preheat the oven to hot 220°C (425°F/
Gas 7). Divide the filling among the
pastry bases and bake for 30 minutes,
or until the custard is set and the tops
have browned. Cool in the tins, then
transfer to a wire rack.

Makes 12

Apricot and coconut macaroons

3 egg whites
1³/₄ cups (435 g) caster sugar
1¹/₄ cups (115 g) desiccated coconut
¹/₂ cup (125 g) finely chopped glacé apricots
1¹/₂ tablespoons plain flour
icing sugar, for dusting

Preheat the oven to slow 150°C (300°F/Gas 2). Line a baking tray with baking paper. Combine the egg whites and sugar in a bowl and place over a saucepan of simmering water over low heat, making sure the base of the bowl does not touch the water. Whisk for about 5 minutes, or until thick and glossy. Do not overheat or the whites will cook. Allow to cool slightly, then fold in the coconut, apricots and flour. Mix well. The mixture should be firm enough to pipe.

Spoon the warm mixture into a large piping bag fitted with a 1 cm plain tube. Pipe 3 cm round mounds on the baking tray, leaving about 3 cm between each mound. With a wet finger, gently press the top down, so it doesn't overbrown during baking.

Bake for about 18–20 minutes or until light brown all over, then cool on the trays. Dust the tops lightly with icing sugar before serving.

Makes about 45

Note: If you don't have a piping bag, use a plastic bag and snip 1 cm off one of the corners; you will probably need to do it in two batches.
Think ahead: The macaroons will keep for up to 3 days if they are stored in an airtight container.

Baby coffee and walnut sour cream cakes

3/4 cup (75 g) walnuts
2/3 cup (155 g) firmly packed soft
  brown sugar
125 g unsalted butter, softened
2 eggs, lightly beaten
1 cup (125 g) self-raising flour
1/3 cup (80 g) sour cream
1 tablespoon coffee and chicory
  essence

Preheat the oven to warm 160°C (315°F/Gas 2–3). Lightly grease two 12-hole 1/4 cup (60 ml) baby muffin tins. Process the walnuts and 1/4 cup (45 g) of the brown sugar in a food processor until the walnuts are roughly chopped into small pieces. Transfer to a bowl.

Cream the butter and remaining sugar together in the food processor until pale and creamy. With the motor running, gradually add the egg and process until smooth. Add the flour and blend until well mixed. Add the sour cream and essence and process until thoroughly mixed.

Spoon half a teaspoon of the walnut and sugar mixture into the base of each muffin hole, followed by a teaspoon of the cake mixture. Sprinkle a little more walnut mixture over the top, a little more cake mixture and top with the remaining walnut mixture. Bake for 20 minutes, or until risen and springy to the touch. Leave in the tins for 5 minutes. Remove the cakes using the handle of a teaspoon to loosen the side and base, then transfer to a wire rack to cool completely.

Makes 24

Chocolate brownies

⅓ cup (40 g) plain flour
½ cup (60 g) cocoa powder
2 cups (500 g) sugar
1 cup (125 g) chopped pecans or
  golden walnuts
250 g dark chocolate
250 g butter
2 teaspoons vanilla essence
4 eggs, lightly beaten

Preheat the oven to moderate 180°C (350°F/Gas 4). Brush a 20 x 30 cm cake tin with melted butter or oil. Line the base with baking paper, extending over the two long sides.

Sift the flour and cocoa into a bowl and add the sugar and nuts. Mix together and make a well.

Using a large sharp knife, chop the chocolate into small pieces and add to the dry ingredients.

Melt the butter in a small pan over low heat and add to the dry ingredients with the vanilla and eggs. Mix well.

Pour into the tin, smooth the surface and bake for 50 minutes (the mixture will still be a bit soft on the inside). Refrigerate for at least 2 hours before cutting and serving.

Makes 24

Note: Use a good-quality chocolate. Cooking chocolate is not suitable for this recipe.

Baklava

Syrup
2 cups (500 g) sugar
2 whole cloves
1 slice lemon
½ teaspoon ground cardamom

1½ cups (235 g) finely chopped
  unblanched almonds
1½ cups (185 g) finely chopped
  walnuts
1 teaspoon ground cardamom
1 teaspoon mixed spice
½ cup (125 g) caster sugar
16 sheets filo pastry
160 g unsalted butter, melted

To make the syrup, put the sugar, cloves, lemon, cardamom and 2 cups (500 ml) of water in a large heavy-based pan and bring to the boil, stirring. Simmer for 12 minutes, remove the cloves and lemon and refrigerate.

Preheat the oven to moderate 180°C (350°F/Gas 4). Grease an 18 x 28 cm shallow tin. Mix the almonds, walnuts, cardamom, mixed spice and sugar in a bowl. Take 4 sheets of filo and, layering the pastry, brush each sheet lightly with some of the melted butter. Fold the sheets in half crossways, trim the edges so the pastry fits the base of the tin, then put in the tin.

Sprinkle one-third of the nut mixture over the filo, then top with another 4 sheets of filo, brushing each with some of the melted butter and then layering, folding and trimming.

Repeat the layers twice more. Trim the edges of the top layers of filo, brush with melted butter and score into large diamonds. Bake for 30–35 minutes, or until golden brown and crisp.

Pour the cold syrup over the hot baklava and refrigerate overnight before cutting into diamonds.

Serves 10

Lemon curd and blueberry tartlets

150 ml lemon juice
2 teaspoons finely grated lemon zest
6 egg yolks
1/2 cup (125 g) sugar
100 g butter, diced
4 sheets ready-made shortcrust
  pastry (24 cm x 24 cm)
2 tablespoons icing sugar
48 blueberries

Whisk together the lemon juice, zest, egg yolks and sugar, then cook in a saucepan over low heat for 2 minutes, or until the sugar has dissolved. Gradually add the butter, stirring continuously, and cook for 10 minutes, or until thick. Remove from the heat and cover the surface with plastic wrap to prevent a skin forming. Refrigerate until needed.

Preheat the oven to moderate 180°C (350°F/Gas 4) and lightly grease 24 x 3 cm tartlet tins. Cut 48 rounds from the pastry with a 5 cm cutter and line the tins with half of them. Lay the other rounds on a lined baking tray, cover with plastic wrap and refrigerate until needed. Bake the cases for 12–15 minutes, or until golden. Allow to cool completely. Repeat with the remaining rounds.

When cool, dust each tartlet with icing sugar and spoon 1 teaspoon curd into each one; top with a blueberry.

Makes 48

Think ahead: The cases can be baked up to 1 week in advance and stored in an airtight container. To revive them, heat in a moderate 180°C (350°F/Gas 4) oven for 5 minutes. The curd can be made 2 days ahead. Assemble the tarts no more than 1 hour before serving.

Fortune cookies

3 egg whites
½ cup (60 g) icing sugar, sifted
45 g unsalted butter, melted
½ cup (60 g) plain flour

Preheat the oven to moderate 180°C (350°F/Gas 4). Lightly grease a baking tray. Draw three 8 cm circles on a sheet of baking paper, turn over and use to line the tray.

Place the egg whites in a clean, dry bowl and whisk until just frothy. Add the icing sugar and butter and stir until smooth. Add the flour, mix until smooth and leave for 15 minutes. Using a flat-bladed knife, spread 2 level teaspoons of mixture over each circle. Bake for 5 minutes, or until the biscuits are slightly brown around the edges.

Working quickly, remove from the trays by sliding a flat-bladed knife under each round. Place a written fortune message in each cookie. Fold in half, then in half again, over the edge of a bowl or a palette knife. Keep a tea towel handy to use when folding the cookies. The tray is hot and you need to work fast, so take care not to burn your hands. Cool on a wire rack. Cook the remaining mixture the same way. Make two or three cookies at a time, otherwise they will harden too quickly and break when folding.

Makes 30

Fennel wafers

¼ cup (60 g) sugar
2 tablespoons sesame seeds
2 tablespoons fennel seeds
1½ cups (185 g) plain flour
¼ cup (60 ml) olive oil
¼ cup (60 ml) beer
1 tablespoon anisette liqueur

Preheat the oven to moderately hot 200°C (400°F/Gas 6). Lightly grease a baking tray and line with baking paper. Combine the sugar, sesame seeds and fennel seeds.

Sift the flour and a pinch of salt into a large bowl and make a well in the centre. Add the oil, beer and liqueur, and mix with a large metal spoon until the dough comes together.

Transfer the dough to a lightly floured surface and knead until elastic. Wrap in plastic wrap and refrigerate for 30 minutes. Divide the dough in two and roll each portion out between two sheets of baking paper as thinly as possible. Stamp rounds out of the dough using a 4 cm round cutter; you should get about 40 rounds.

Sprinkle the dough rounds with the sugar mixture, then gently roll a rolling pin over the top of them so that the seeds adhere to the dough.

Transfer the rounds to a baking tray and cook for 6–8 minutes. Put the wafers under a hot grill for 2 minutes to caramelise the sugar, taking care not to burn them. Transfer to a wire rack and allow to cool.

Makes about 40

Index

INDEX

INDEX

Photographers: Cris Cordeiro, Craig Cranko, Joe Filshie, Roberto Jean François, Ian Hofstetter, Andre Martin, Rob Reichenfeld, Brett Stevens

Food Stylists: Marie-Hélène Clauzon, Jane Collins, Sarah de Nardi, Georgina Dolling, Cherise Koch, Michelle Noerianto

Food Preparation: Alison Adams, Justine Johnson, Valli Little, Ben Masters, Kate Murdoch, Kim Passenger, Justine Poole, Christine Sheppard, Angela Tregonning

Published by Murdoch Books® a division of Murdoch Magazines Pty Ltd,
GPO Box 1203, Sydney NSW 1045

Editorial Director: Diana Hill. Editor: Katharine Gasparini
Creative Director: Marylouise Brammer. Designer: Annette Fitzgerald
Food Directors: Lulu Grimes, Jane Lawson
Photographer (chapter openers): Ian Hofstetter. Stylist (chapter openers): Cherise Koch
Picture Librarian: Genevieve Huard

Chief Executive: Juliet Rogers
Publisher: Kay Scarlett
Production Manager: Kylie Kirkwood

National Library of Australia Cataloguing-in-Publication Data: Small Food. Includes index.
ISBN 1 74045 172 4. 1. Appetizers. 2. Snack Foods.
641.812

Printed by Tien Wah Press
PRINTED IN SINGAPORE

You may find cooking times vary depending on the oven you are using. For fan-forced ovens,
as a general rule, set the oven temperature to 20°C lower than indicated in the recipe.
We have used 20 ml tablespoon measures. If you are using a 15 ml tablespoon, for most recipes
the difference will not be noticeable. However, for recipes using small amounts of flour and cornflour,
add an extra teaspoon for each tablespoon specified. We have used 60 g (Grade 3) eggs in all recipes.

IMPORTANT: Those who might be at risk from the effects of salmonella poisoning (the elderly, pregnant
women, young children and those suffering from immune deficiency diseases) should consult their GP
with any concerns about eating raw eggs.

Published by:	UK
AUSTRALIA	Murdoch Books® UK
Murdoch Books® Australia	Ferry House
GPO Box 1203	51–57 Lacy Road
Sydney NSW 1045	Putney, London SW15 1PR
Phone: (612) 4352 7000	Phone: (020) 8355 1480
Fax: (612) 4352 7026	Fax: (020) 8355 1499

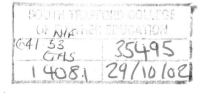